PULLING DOWN
OF
STRONGHOLDS

PULLING DOWN OF STRONGHOLDS

Dr. FRANCIS MADZIVADONDO

*The pulling down of strongholds
is not the work of God to perform...*

Pulling Down of Strongholds
Published by Dr Francis Madzivadondo
New Zealand

© 2020 Francis Madzivadondo

ISBN 978-0-473-53429-5 (Softcover)
ISBN 978-0-473-53430-1 (ePUB)
ISBN 978-0-473-53431-8 (Kindle)

Editing:
Knowledge Mawere

Production & Typesetting:
Andrew Killick
Castle Publishing Services
www.castlepublishing.co.nz

Cover design:
Karel Makombe and Taffy Musoni

Scripture quotations are taken from
The Authorised (King James) Version.
Rights in the Authorised Version in the United Kingdom
are vested in the Crown.
Reproduced by permission of the Crown's patentee,
Cambridge University Press.

ALL RIGHTS RESERVED

No part of this publication may be reproduced,
stored in a retrieval system, or transmitted
in any form or by any means, electronic, mechanical,
photocopying, recording or otherwise,
without prior written permission from the author.

(For the weapons of our warfare are not canal but are mighty through God to the pulling down of strongholds;) Casting down imaginations, and every high thing that exalts itself against the knowledge of God, and bringing into captivity every thought to the obedience of Christ. (2 Corinthians 10:4-5)

ACKNOWLEDGEMENTS

Thanks for this book must be given and expressed to my dear wife Sandra and my five children, Evans, Blessing, Nyasha, Tinotenda and Tinashe and their children for the encouragement that they gave me as I was writing this book. They provided a conducive atmosphere that allowed me to be able to hear from God to be able to write the book.

Professor Ezekiel Guti and Dr Eunor Guti the Apostles of Jesus Christ, the founders of Forward In Faith Ministries International for mentoring me and moulding me into a minister of the Gospel of Jesus Christ. I thank them for their patience with me over the years as I was growing up in the work of the ministry.

Dr Steve Simukai, during our formative years at bible college we used to talk about writing a combined book and that remained at the back of my mind all the years and God has given me the grace. I believe this is the road map to that vision of having a combined book. Thank you for the encouragement.

Forward In Faith Ministries International church in Lubumbashi DRC. This is where everything began about the writing of this book. Most of the things in this book I first taught them to the church as the Lord was giving me revelation. Thank you for all the support that you used to give me.

Forward In Faith Ministries International church in Brisbane Australia. Thank you for your support and those prayers that we used to do together.

Reason Wafawarova and Musa Chiboora these guys did a wonderful job of proof-reading my manuscripts.

I give all the glory to my Father God for giving me the ability to write this book. Teachers at school used to tell me that I was not that sharp enough. I thank my Father God who has delivered me from thinking that I cannot do much. Writing a book was one of those things that I thought I could never do. I now know that with God I can do all things through Christ who strengthens me. Thank you, Lord!!!!

CONTENTS

Preface: A Personal Reflection and Revelation   11

Introduction   15

1. What is a Stronghold?   23

2. How are Strongholds Built?   29
   - Parents   32
   - Schools and Other School Children   35
   - Friends   42
   - Politicians and Traditional Leaders   43
   - Cultures and Traditions   45
   - Religion   48
   - Media   52

3. Types of Strongholds   57
   - The Stronghold of Fear   57
   - The Stronghold of Sickness   61
   - The Stronghold of Sexual Immorality   66
   - The Stronghold of Poverty   67

4. How are Strongholds Destroyed?   73
   - The Word of God   74
   - Faith   86

The Blood of Jesus Christ	92
Prayer and Fasting	94
The Name of Jesus Christ	98
The Holy Spirit	100
The Fivefold Ministry	102
5. Conclusion	105
Bibliography and References	115
About the Author	117

PREFACE

A PERSONAL REFLECTION AND REVELATION

The writing of this book came because of much reflection on thoughts that bothered me. The bible has promises that God has outlined and how children of God should live but generally I have seen that many are not living lives that measure to the promises. Numbers 23:19 "God is not a man, that He should lie; neither the son of man, that he should repent: hath he said, and shall he not do it? Or hath he spoken, and shall he not make it good?" This assured me that the problem was not with God but with us children of God and the Holy Spirit started to teach me about strongholds.

God has promised abundant life according to John 10:10 "The thief cometh not, but for to steal, and to kill, and to destroy: I am come that they might have life, and that they might have it more abundantly." Many of us children of God seem to move to a certain level in our lives both spiritually and materially and then we get into a stagnation mode. The excitement of salvation slowly dies down until it's all gone in many people. Some backslide, some soldier on and continue to go to church with virtually nothing spiritual happening in the inside of them and they become religious. The word of God is no longer taken as truth that can transform lives. Scriptures are read and quoted here and there but with no faith.

Songs of victory continue to be sung in church services and

everybody is acting victorious but after the service when we go back to our homes, many are victims of demons. If you talk one on one with someone you then discover how oppressed they are and how hopeless and discouraged.

These observations made me to want to enquire more from the Lord and know more from Him. God is true, why then these stagnations? I started to pray and fast about it and search the scriptures. The answer took some years to come but I continued with my search until I got something. This is not all but it's part of the biggest contributor of stagnation.

I discovered that, yes, one can get born again but can continue under the oppression, suppression of demons and strongholds. It does not matter your rank in the church or the years that you have been in church, you must confront certain issues in your life. One cannot confront things that he is not aware of. When a person gets born again, what gets born again is his spirit. His flesh and mind are not born again and his way of thinking is still the same. His wrong way of thinking will soon be a problem to his spirit which is now born again. His spirit is thinking in line with the word of God, but the mind is against the word of God. The spiritual perspective of the spirit is different from that of the flesh. The spirit man is spiritually focused, but the mind is worldly focused. Galatians 5:17 "For the flesh lusteth against the spirit, and the spirit against the flesh: and these are contrary the one to the other: so that ye cannot do the things that ye would."

After spiritual birth one must deliver his mindset, it is through the mind that the devil binds people. Our mindset has power to bind us even if we are children of God. There is nothing that God can do about this. One must deliver himself with the weapons and tools that God has provided. This is my job to do and not God. God did his part, now it is my turn to set myself free. Our lives are controlled by what is happening in our minds and demons influence us through the mind. Everything that we see, hear, touch, smell etc is processed in the mind and the mind gives the final say. The mind is the major door that demons use to enter a man.

Romans 12:2 "And be not conformed to this world; but be transformed by the renewing of your mind, that ye may prove what is that good, and acceptable, and perfect, will of God." Transformation of the mind is not done by God but by you and me. This is where the rubber meets the road. Many children of God do not invest time in the word of God. They think what they hear from the Pastor on Sunday is enough, but this is not enough to change your mindset.

Many times, people are not being troubled by demons but by strongholds. Strongholds are built in a person from the day that person is born. Those strongholds are so effective that they give enough trouble to people and paralyse their lives, and demons can then come in and out at their pleasure. They do not have to be in a man permanently. Therefore, when you try to cast a demon of poverty from a man many times there is no manifestation of any demon and yet the man is in poverty. What it means is a stronghold of poverty has been built in the mindset of that person.

When a demon is cast out and the stronghold is not destroyed the demon will always have access to come back and occupy its victim through the stronghold. Matthew 12:43-44 "When the unclean spirit is gone out of a man, he walketh through dry places, seeking rest, and findeth none. Then he saith, I will return into my house from whence I came out; and when he is come, he findeth it empty, swept and garnished. Then goeth he, and taketh with himself seven other spirits more wicked than himself, and the last state of that man is worse than the first.

Even so shall it be also unto this wicked generation." The demon says let me go to my house. If the house is destroyed the demon will go and cannot come back again.

Casting out demons from someone and not destroy the stronghold is a job halfway done and causes the state of the person to be worse than his first state. Strongholds are the primary reasons many are not experiencing the abundant kind of life that God has promised us.

Let us now take a journey into studying and get understanding about strongholds.

INTRODUCTION

In this book I am trying to bring to light to someone who is wondering why his life has come to a standstill, spiritually and physically. Sometimes, people engage themselves in some breakthrough kind of prayer bands trying to make a frantic effort to bring movement, change in their lives. Prayer bands are good but on their own without dealing with your thoughts and mind you will accomplish very little. If you go into prayer with a wrong mindset, it does not help you much. How you pray is guided by how you think and what you know about God. If you have a wrong mindset you will pray wrongly. In most cases the devil will push you to pray but praying for the wrong thing and not the right way. He causes you to pray and fast where you are not supposed to be praying. He makes you use the tools that God has provided but wrongly. Where you need the word of God, he leads you to pray. Where you need to pray, he influences you to read the word.

Pulling down of stronghold is not the work of God to do but it is my job to do. Unfortunately, most of us have been waiting for God to set us free. John 8:31-32 "Then said Jesus to those Jews which believed on Him, if ye continue in my word, then ye are my disciples indeed; And ye shall know the truth, and the truth shall make you free." You set yourself free by the word of God. God finished His part at Calvary that is why He said, it is finished. John 19:28-30 "After this, Jesus knowing that all things were now accomplished, that the scripture might be fulfilled, saith, I thirst. Now there was a set a vessel full of vinegar; and they filled a spunge with vinegar, and put it hyssop, and put it to His mouth. When Jesus therefore received the vinegar, He said, it is finished: and He bowed His head, and gave up the ghost."

The devil is interested on our minds. Once he gets hold of our minds, then he is through with us. Everything about you is controlled in your mind. The more the mind is bound, the spirit man is muffled he cannot operate the way God made him to operate. Strongholds may be passed on from generation to generation just as diseases are passed on. The devil uses cultures and traditions to build strongholds. People live by principles of their cultures and traditions instead of the word of God. Matthew 4:4 "But He answered them and said, man shall not live by bread alone, but by every word that proceedeth out of the mouth of God."

The pulling down of strongholds is not the work of God to perform, but rather it is the work of an individual to do using the weapons that God has given to us. The weapons include:

- The blood of Jesus Christ
- Faith
- The Word of God
- The power of the Holy Spirit
- Prayer and fasting
- The name of Jesus Christ
- The five-fold ministry

2 Corinthians 10:4-5 "For the weapons of our warfare are not canal, but they are mighty through God to the pulling down of strongholds, casting down imaginations, and every high thing that exalts itself against the knowledge of the word of God, and bring into captivity every thought to the obedience of Christ."

Introduction

The pulling down of a stronghold in one's life is not a one-day job. It is progressive and it takes time. When they are being built by demons it's not a one day's job either – it starts from the time a child is born. Many tools are used to build strongholds, and they are built by the strongman, the devil and a host of his demons. After strongholds are built then demons launch their attacks through the strongholds, and the devil's power in people's lives lies in the strongholds. These strongholds have power to paralyse the ability and the potential that God has placed in a human being and frustrate God's plan.

The reason why the devil could not succeed in tempting Jesus Christ was because there was no stronghold in His mind. John 14:30 "Hereafter I not talk much with you; for the ruler of this world is coming, and he has nothing in me." The devil can hold you down because he has something that is his that is in you.

The devil is not worried much when people go to church, if they are not aware of his presence in their lives, through some strongholds that he has established. Without strongholds in my life the devil has no power over me.

The mind is very powerful, no one can live above what he thinks. Man is a product of his thinking and the objective of the devil is to attack the mind. Proverbs 23:7 "For as he thinketh in his heart, so is he; eat and drink, saith he to thee; but his heart is not with thee." The mind controls everything that a man does and every function of the body is attached to the mind. David Lahaye and David Noebel, *Mind Siege*, page 48 "The way you think is the result of the intellectual you inherited plus your training, plus what you have seen, read, done and heard. The philosophy of life that you adopt on the basis of what you have programmed into your mind through your reason, and your study determines the way you look at life. This affects your morals, work drive, and life investment." The devil is in the business of polluting the mind and when the mind is polluted the whole person is polluted.

An established stronghold is a series of lies that people uphold as truth and they base their lives on it. It becomes a window of opportunity through which demons can manipulate the lives of people. A stronghold causes people to reject the word of God, unless one is delivered by the Lord Jesus Christ, and it gives people a false foundation which man begins to live upon. In the world that we are living today, it is normal or even fashionable to reject the truth of the word of God, and life is built on a false foundation. The false foundation is the lack of knowledge which is spoken about by God through prophet Hosea. Hosea 4:6 "My people are destroyed for lack of knowledge; because thou hast rejected knowledge, I will also reject thee, that thou shalt be no priest to me: seeing thou hast forgotten the law of thy God, I will also forget thy children."

The lie that the devil wants to be entrenched in the mindset of man is that the problems and challenges of this world which he creates are so overwhelming that failure is inevitable. He wants people to think that they cannot control their own destinies and cannot change anything in their lives, while the truth is that man has the capacity to change every circumstance that may come his way through Christ Jesus. The word of God is the truth which people must believe, and in the word God says that man can do all things through Christ Jesus – he is limitless. Philippians 4:13 "I can do all things through Christ who strengthens me."

This assurance is what renders powerless the power of strongholds. Strongholds paralyse the potential that God has put in man since the foundation of the world. Genesis 1:26-28 "And God said, let us make man in our image, after our likeness;

and let them have dominion over the fish of the sea, and over the fowl of the air, and over the cattle, and over all the earth, and over every creeping thing that creepeth upon the earth. God created man in His own image, in the image of God created he him; male and female created He them. And God blessed them, and God said unto them, be fruitful, and multiply, replenish the earth, and subdue it; and have dominion over the fish of the sea, and over the fowl of the air, and over every living thing that moveth upon the earth." When God blessed man, he gave him capacity to do all things, gave him the potential to do all things if he lived according to the will of God.

The devil has set standards in the world to define success, and everyone who does not match those standards is automatically disqualified. This success, for the most part is linked to academic success. If one fails academically, he is deemed a failure in life. Being successful academically does not mean one is going to be a success story in life. Life is more than academia, life is with God not in the number of academic degrees that someone has. Proverbs 8:35 " For whosoever findeth me findeth life, and shall obtain favour of the Lord." God has put success and prosperity in you. Joshua 1:8 "This book of the law shall not depart out of thy mouth; but thou shalt meditate therein day and night, that thou mayest observe to do according to all that is written therein: for then thou shalt make thy way prosperous, and then thou shalt have good success."

Great damage than what people realise has been done to the belief system of man. What people call normal is not normal at all and what they believe to be true is not true. Romans 1:24-25 "Wherefore God also gave them up to uncleanness through the lusts of their own hearts, to dishonour their own bodies between themselves: Who changed the truth of God into a lie and worshipped and saved the creature more than the creator, who is blessed forever." The devil knows that if he corrupts the mindset of a man, he has destroyed him.

The mind of a man is mysteriously connected to the heart of a man which is his spirit. Sometimes the heart stands for the mind and in some instances, it stands for the spirit of a man. The spirit and soul together can be referred to us the heart of a man. The two spirit and soul cannot be separated. When a man dies these two leave the body and they go back to God. Ecclesiastes 12:7 "Then the dust returns to the earth as it was: and the spirit shall return unto God who gave it." When a man dies his spirit and his soul go back to God. The mind and the spirit are closely linked. They have direct connection and influence on each other. They are indispensable and cannot be separated.

The mind is the gateway into the spirit of a man, and when something gets into the mind it must be transferred into the spirit. For example, when one gets angry that starts in the mind but as the man continues to think or meditate what has happened that anger is transferred into the spirit and it develops into bitterness. Bitterness is more dangerous and very difficult to deal with than anger, that is why the word of God says that we should not let the sun go down in our anger. If we spend long hours in anger it develops into bitterness and bitterness becomes a stronghold that attracts demons in your life. Proverbs 4:26 "Be angry, and do not sin do not let the sun go down on your wroth."

Man cannot live above what he thinks – he is his thoughts, and if his thoughts or mind has been fed with wrong stuff he will live wrongly. He gets wrong settings in his life, therefore everything about him will be wrong. The disbelief in man is a stronghold and was done deliberately by the devil so that man would suffer for the rest of his life. The disbelief did not start on its own, it was a result of lies that were taught that are contrary to the word of God. God's plan about man is that he should live in abundance. Jeremiah 29:11 "For I know the plans that I have towards you, saith the Lord, thoughts of peace, and not of evil, to give you an expected end." John 10:10 "The thief cometh not, but for to steal, and to kill, and to destroy I am come that they might have life, and that they might have it more abundantly." The plan of God is for us to have abundance in every domain of our lives, and that we must realise full potential in all that we do without any limits.

Man is failing to reach his full potential because he has accepted the lies of the enemy as the truth and is living and operating upon them. The purpose of strongholds is to bind man strongly so that he may not live life fully according to the plan of God. The strongholds regulate, limit and control its victim, therefore, man is not operating fully – his potential and ability has been thwarted. Many people are dying with all their potential untapped because of strongholds. They have the feeling that they are not able to do what they want to do – they feel limited. Many could have done things that could have changed the world for the better but because of strongholds their visions only ended up in dreams. People are full of inventions and ideas locked up in them, but they are not able to unleash them, all is in the mind. Many times people think they are oppressed and suppressed by other men but many times its these strongholds.

CHAPTER 1

WHAT IS A STRONGHOLD?

A stronghold does not allow advancement or progress to take place in the right direction. One is held by force mentally, even if there is the desire to move forward. The person is bound beyond his ability to get loose.

From the biblical point of view a stronghold is a twist of the truth – a lie that is construed as truth and people live by it, a negative belief that becomes action and the character of a person. It is a twist or distortion, misrepresentation of the word of God and the true principles of the word of God. Every teaching that is contrary to the word of God will always create strongholds in man. Genesis 3:4-6 "And the serpent said unto the woman, ye shall not surely die: For God doth know that in the day ye eat thereof, then your eyes shall be opened, and ye shall be as gods, knowing good and evil. And when the woman saw that the tree was good for food, and that it was pleasant to the eyes, and the tree to be desired to make one wise, she took of the fruit thereof, and eat and gave also unto her husband with her; and he did eat." Man was created by God to live by His word and not by any other teaching or belief. Matthew 4:4 "But He answered and said it is written, man shall not live by bread alone, but by every word that proceedeth out of the mouth of God."

A stronghold is the lie of the devil that is fed into the mind of a person and the person starts to live life according to that lie, and the standard of his life is based upon the lie and not upon the word of God which is a sure foundation.

The devil uses strongholds to fight the truth of the word of God. They are built in the mind of a person by demons and the devil, through humanistic, demonic, satanic, diabolic teachings that are contrary to the word of God. Tim Lahaye and David Noebel, *Mind Siege*, page 48. "Life is mainly about the battle of your mind, whether you live upon man's wisdom or by the wisdom of God." 1 Corinthians 1:17-25 "For Christ sent me not to baptize, but to preach the gospel; not with wisdom of words, lest the cross of Christ should be made of none effect. For the preaching of the cross is to them that perish foolishness; but unto us which are saved it is the power of God. For it is written, I will destroy the wisdom of the wise, and will bring to nothing the understanding of the prudent. Where is the wise? Where is the scribe? Where is the disputer of this word? Hath God not made foolish the wisdom of this world? For after that in the wisdom of God the world by wisdom knew not God, it pleased God by the foolishness of preaching to save them that believe. For the Jews require a sign, and Greeks seek after wisdom: But we preach Christ crucified, unto the Jews a stumblingblock, and unto the Greeks foolishness; But unto them which are called both Jews and Greeks, Christ the power of God, and the wisdom of God. Because the foolishness of God is wiser than men; and the weakness of God is stronger than man."

The devil knows that the mind of a man is the workshop that determines man's choices and actions in life, and he uses strongholds to hold back every move of man towards his godly destiny. The building of these strongholds starts from the time one is born. He starts to manipulate the mind of the child through worldly systems that he has put in place. Romans 12:2

"And be not confirmed to this world: but be ye transformed by the renewing of your mind, that ye may prove what is that good, and acceptable, and perfect, will of God."

The bible is very clear about the systems of this world being controlled by the devil. 1 John 5:19 "And we know that we are of God, and the whole world lieth in wickedness." John 12:31 "Now is the judgement of this world: now shall the prince of this world be cast out." The world is being run by a system founded on the lies of the devil, and those lies are used to shape the laws of the world and the mindset of the people. The devil who is running this world is a liar. John 8:44 "Ye are of your father the devil, and the lusts of your father ye will do. He was a murderer from the beginning, and abode not in the truth, because there is no truth in him. When he speaketh a lie he speaketh of his own: for he is a liar, and the father of it."

A significant amount of what we call facts and truth is nothing but the opinion of man that is often based on the lie upon which the devil controls the world from. The measure against which we determine this lie is the word of God as written in the bible. Any information valued by man as knowledge or truth but is contrary to the word of God is a lie of the devil.

When one internalises values that contradict the word of God, those values will begin to shape the beliefs of that person, and those beliefs become the strongholds that the devil uses to control his thoughts and mind. The world order of governance today is reliant not upon the teachings of the word of God but based on what man views in his own sophisticated wisdom and intelligence. The worldly systems I am talking about cover most of the ordinary facets of society including but not limited to the following:

- The Economic System

- The accepted Cultures and Traditions that are sold to societies
- The Justice Systems
- The Educational Systems
- The Health Systems
- The Religious and Political Systems

Ordinary people do not see anything wrong with all these systems. They seem very innocent. They seem to be helping society, yet they are enemies of humanity. You need the eye of God to understand what I am saying. All these and others that I have not mentioned are there to bombard the mind of man. This is the machinery that the devil, and his demons use to build strongholds.

A society that does not base its values on the righteousness of the kingdom of God will teach its people to rely on the systems of the world masterminded by satan himself. A child raised in this environment has a body of knowledge that places values on issues that corrupt societies. This creates a cycle of ignorance, and a culture where evil is considered good, heresies and lies are accepted as truth. The devil is inherently a liar and he thrives on spreading lies to keep people in deception and disillusioned. It takes the salvation of the cross of Jesus Christ to discover the lies of the devil.

A stronghold is the lie inherent in an environment of ungodliness, a lie found on a body of knowledge built in a man's system from birth through all the nurturing phases of life. The lies of the devil get transformed into lifestyles of people, and at this point man defines his way of living based on a norm of deception and lies. The lie of the devil can be traced back to the garden of Eden. Genesis 3:4-5 "And the serpent said unto the woman, ye shall not surely die; For God doth know that in the day ye eat thereof, then your eyes shall be opened, and ye shall be as gods, knowing good and evil." When the lie of the devil is established as the pillar of societal values a stronghold has been built in the minds of the people who believe that lie and live by it. Demons are always busy building strongholds. Some of the strongholds are passed on from generation to generation through culture, education and traditions.

CHAPTER 2

HOW ARE STRONGHOLDS BUILT?

Strongholds are built by satan and his demons and this is their work on a fulltime basis. Once strongholds are built, demons have the power to control the life of a person even without any demon present. Strongholds can operate with demons or with no demon present and they are stronger than demons. When you cast out a demon from someone and you do not destroy the stronghold the demon will come back without any problem and repossess the person. Matthew 12:43-45 "When the unclean spirit is gone out of a man, he walketh through dry places, seeking rest, and findeth none. Then he saith, I will return into my house from whence I came out, and when he is come, he findeth it empty, swept, and garnished. Then goeth he, and taketh with himself, and they enter in and dwell there; and last state of that man is worse than the first."

The culture and belief systems of the world are used by the devil and his demons to establish strongholds that derail God's plan for man's life. He uses lifetime strategies that he applies from the day a child is born until the day he breathes his last breath on earth. The strategies include devious deception, false doctrines, and vain philosophies all designed to make man pursue vanity. For example, the theory of evolution – demons are making people believe that the world came into being through a big bang, not that it was created by God. Ecclesiastes 1:14 "I have seen all the works that are done under the sun; and behold, all is vanity and vexation of spirit." Many laws that are governing the world are influenced by deception of the devil and that is why the world is increasingly finding it easy to legalise immorality and outright abominations.

Prostitution, homosexuality and fornication, are well spelt iniquity in the word of God. Leviticus 20:13-17 "If a man also lie with mankind, as he lieth with woman, both of them have committed abomination: they shall surely be put to death, their blood shall be upon them. And if a man takes her mother as awife, it is wickedness; they shall be burnt with fire, both he and they; that there be no wickedness among you. And if a man lie with a beast, he shall surely be put to death; and ye shall slay the beast. And if a woman approach unto any beast, and lie down thereto, thou shalt kill the woman, and the beast; they shall surely be put to death; their blood shall be upon them. And if a man shall take his sister, his father's daughter, or his mother's daughter, and see her nakedness, and she see his nakedness; it is a wicked thing; and they shall be cut off in the sight of their people: he hath uncovered his sister's nakedness; he shall bear his iniquity." 1 Corinthians 6:9 " Know ye not that the unrighteous shall not inherit the kingdom of God? Be not deceived; neither fornicaters, nor adulterers, nor effeminate, nor abusers of themselves with mankind, nor thieves, nor covetous, nor drunkards, nor revlers, nor extortioners, shall inherit the kingdom of God." Romans 1:26-28 "For this cause God gave them up unto vile affections; for even their women did change the natural use into that which is against nature; And likewise also men, leaving the natural use of the woman, burned in their lust one toward another; men with men working that which is unseemly, and receiving in themselves that recompence of their error which was meet. And even as they did not like to retain God in their knowledge, God gave them over to a reprobate mind, to do those things which are not convenient."

Today these practices stand legalised in many countries of the world in the name of civilization and freedom. Man was not created to live according to the gospel of civilization but according to the word of God. Civilization is man made with the influence of the devil. The devil makes man explain sin and understand sin to the point that not only of tolerating it but also legalising it and even employs the police force to enforce the committing of such sin. For example, if you try to speak against homosexuality you get into trouble – there are established world bodies, so called freedom bodies that protect such people.

The devil is running the world, and has put in place strategies and tools that he needs in building strongholds. The strategies are there ready to feed false doctrines, and human philosophies into the fresh mind of every child who is born into the world. The child is born into a corrupt world with laws that are contrary to the word of God. He accepts everything because he is born into an abnormal society, but he is ignorant of the fact – he takes all that he sees adults doing and he thinks all is well. As he takes all that he is learning, strongholds are being built in his mind and these things will cripple his life as he grows up. The child is not aware that he has been born into a perverse and crooked society. Deuteronomy 32:5 "They have corrupted themselves; their spot is not the spot of his children; they are a perverse and crooked generation." Governments of the world make laws, but those laws have the influence of the devil, and those who make the laws are not even aware of the influence of the devil.

Parents

In the absence of true salvation, parents are the first target that the devil uses to spoil the mind of a child. They are the first to be used to build strongholds in the child's mind, since they are the first teachers of children. Parents who are themselves victims of the devil's deception will naturally pass on the values of deception to their children, unless that cycle is broken by true salvation through Jesus Christ. The cycle can continue to affect lineages from generation to generation. If parents of a child have been nurtured and taught by the way of the world, it follows that they will pass it on to their children only that which is inherent within them.

"It is that many children suffer mentally and physically because of ungodly parents. It is true that blessings follow generations of God-fearing parents. The influence that parents have for good or evil is greater than they realize. Parents who are not Christian, who do not worship God, do not read the bible and have no family worship in their homes, are not doing their duties before God and to their children. Parents need to be alert to evil spirits that will influence their children. Parents need to be alert to evil spirits that will influence children. Evil spirits are subtle and destructive and will try to control a young child's heart. Whenever these are established in a child's life, they are very difficult to control." *A Superb Handbook for Successful Living*, page 12, by Robert H. Givons, AuthorHouse.

There is often a replication of certain habits within families, for example some families produce a series of thieves while others produce habitual liars and so forth. This is largely a result of parents playing the wrong role model to their children. In the absence of the plan of God a child is left to grow according to the plan of the devil.

When a child is a victim of the devious deception of the

devil, it does not mean that he worships the devil. Naturally most people grow up seriously resentful of the devil. There is always an inherent desire to belong to God and an almost natural inclination to hate evil. The problem comes when the devil hides himself in what people value most in their lives. He hides in people's lifestyles, in what they want to think, in politics of nations and even in religion. Paul was religiously brought up in a way that made him to resent and persecute the real followers of Jesus Christ. Acts 22:3-4 "I am verily a man which am a Jew born in Tarsus, a city in Cilicia, yet brought up in this city at the feet of Gamaliel and Taught according to the perfect manner of the law of the fathers, and was zealous toward, as ye all are this day. And I persecuted this way unto death, binding and delivering into prisons both men and women." He thought he was doing a great service to God according to the way he was taught since he was a child. Paul did not hate God he loved God, but the problem was the way the teachers taught him. The teachers were under the influence of demons. A stronghold of religion was built in his mind.

This is the pattern of strongholds in deceiving people for purposes of making them depart from the will of God thinking that they are serving God. It is important in the analysis of strongholds to keep focusing on why the devil finds it important to target young children in this deception plan. The simple truth is that they are young and vulnerable, they are unpolluted still fresh therefore are easy targets for deception. When parents themselves have been deceived the life of a newly born child is dangerously exposed to the manipulation of the powers of darkness, and it is the plan of the devil to perpetuate sin and pervasion for as long as there is life on this planet.

Parents innocently pass on to the child the same lies that they received from their parents and society. The parents are unaware that what they are passing on to their children is not the truth. The child starts to fear everything the parents fear. The victories of his parents are his victories, and it is the same with their weaknesses. In all this the child is being trained not to be like God and to see things not the way God sees – he sees everything the way man sees and is being conformed to the standards of the world. Romans 12:2 "And be not conformed to this world: but be ye transformed by the renewing of your mind, that ye may prove what is the good, and perfect, will of God." That is the foundation that is being firmly built in the child which will cause him later in life to refuse to believe what God says – a foundation of strongholds is built in the mind of a child, instead of Christ. Ephesians 2:19-22 "Now therefore ye are no more strangers and foreigners, but fellow citizens with the saints, and of the household of God; And are built upon the foundation of the apostles and prophets, Jesus Christ himself being the chief cornerstone; In whom all the building fitly framed together growth unto an holy temple in the Lord; in whom ye also are builded together for an habitation of God through the Spirit."

The parents are used without them knowing. Hosea 4:6 "My people are destroyed for lack of knowledge: because thou hast rejected knowledge, I will also reject thee, that thou shalt be no priest to me: seeing thou hast forgotten the law of thy God, I will also forget thy children." They think they are giving their children wisdom. Vermon Sparks in his book *Child and Education*, page 158, says "Mistaken parents are teaching their children lessons which will prove ruinous to them and are also planting thorns for their own feet." The devil is training the child through parents to have a worldly mindset and that is a stronghold and with this kind of mindset then the devil has ability and capacity to control lives.

The devil uses the ignorant parents, who are ignorant of God, first to pollute and corrupt the mind of a child because he is not yet exposed to the world. The first people the child meet nearest to him are the parents and the child is naturally attached to them. The devil takes advantage of this and straight away launches his attack upon the child. Parents can pass on to even their unborn child the rejection that they have suffered themselves, some diseases etc. "So let parents know that they do not live to themselves alone as mortal but that their evil thoughts and deeds have greater or lesser influence upon the spiritual nature of their children, especially at the time of conception and during gestation." James E. Padgett, *Communications from the Spirit World*, page 147, Lulu Com, 21/07/2008. Every child believes his parents hundred percent. Whatever they tell him the child captures and put it into practice. My parents were heroes when I was a child, I believed in them totally.

Schools and Other School Children
After parents the next person who has a greater impact on the mind of a child is the teacher. A child believes that his teacher knows it all and he is poised to learn everything that the teacher tells him.

The devil has invaded the world educational system for the purpose of building strongholds in the minds of the children through deceptive teachings that are contrary to the word of God. In most schools, colleges, universities all over the world the bible has been taken out of the classroom – there is no room for it. Children may learn all these other subjects but not the word of God. There is someone who hates the word of God and does not want our children to discover who they are, where they came from and who is their maker and for what purpose they were put into the world. He does not want the children to know where they are going. "America's public education is purposely designed to eradicate Jesus Christ from the scene and replace Him with the likes of John Dewey, Sigmund Freud, William Wundt, Fredrich Nietzsche, Karl Marx, Charles Darwin and many more." Tim Lahaye and David Noebel, *Mind Siege*, page 115. "In contemplating the political institutions of the United States, I lament that (if we remove the bible from schools) we waste so much time and money in punishing crimes and take so little pains to prevent them." Christian Van Horn, Xulon Press 2010, page 184.

Many schools that started with the study of bible knowledge have in the name of civil rights abandoned even the reading of the bible. "Dewey succeeded in stripping from American education its final vestiges of the Christian message and purpose." Tim Lahaye and Noebel, *Mind Siege*, page 114. This is the systematic way by which the devil has planted in the education system values contrary to the word of God and the will of God.

The devil has managed to destroy the real reason and purpose why schools were started in the first place. Many schools today that are government owned in many countries were started by God fearing people. Many schools started as seminaries where young people were taught the word of God. The devil influenced governments of the world to take over these schools. We need the teaching of the word of God in our schools now more than ever before. "As the twenty- first century began many wondered what the future would hold. Some have felt that advances in technology have now more than ever created a need for religious and moral instruction of all children. The availability of almost unlimited content on the internet is a concern for many parents." Alan Marzilli, *Religion in Public Schools*, pages 92-93.

Peer pressure in schools is a very powerful tool that the devil uses to cause all children to conform to his standards. There are always the naughty but very influential children whose untoward behaviour easily spread across the school populace like an infectious disease. Demons use these children to ensure mass deception of children in and even out of the school system – it is called peer pressure, but these are demons at work.

I have already said that less and less schools still teach the word of God in the schools across the globe. Where it is still being taught the approach has shifted from doctrinal and spiritual into analytical. Children are being trained to critically analyse the sense that is in all that is written in the word according to man's mental understanding. The bible is not a book of the mind it is a spiritual book that one needs to understand spiritually with the help of the Holy Spirit. If one uses his natural mind the word of God is foolishness. 1 Corinthians 2:14 "But the natural man receiveth not the things of the spirit of God: for they are foolishness unto him; and he cannot know them because they are spiritually discerned." "Man-centred literature took over most of the colleges and universities on the continent, preaching with missionary zeal its prejudices of no God, no Masters, no Absolute but self-sufficient and self-indulgent man." Tim Lahaye and David Noebel, *Mind Siege*, page 111. In the past many churches or missionary schools taught the word of God, not as a mere social subject, but to train and to give value of the Christian doctrine to children.

"It is not overstatement to declare that most of today's evils can be traced to Secular Humanism, which already has taken over our government, the United Nations, education, television and most of the other power centres of life. Secular Humanism - whether it calls itself Marxist Humanism, Scientific Humanism, Planetary Humanism, Postmodern Humanism, or sports some other label is driven by a flaming hatred for Jesus Christ that seeks to eradicate the Christian worldview from the media, the government, and especially public education." Tim Lahaye and David Noebel, *Mind Siege*, page 35. All these secular humanistic organizations were started by the devil and are driven by the him and his demons in order to bring strange doctrines that are against Christ.

Creation as a teaching explaining the origin and the identity of man has been side-lined in the name of science, and the sad result of this unfortunate shift is that the child of today has lost his spiritual sense of identity, together with the spiritual body of knowledge that defines the inner man. When children explain the origin of humanity by the theory of evolution, the biggest challenge is that the theory does not in itself give an identity to the child, rather it centres on the transformation of apes into human beings, and what all that does is to make a child identify with ancient apes and there is no spiritual dimension to that kind of identity. It is so scientific in approach that it tends to treat humanity as mere objects in a science laboratory. The evolution theory is a stronghold that is being used to drive people away from God. Isaiah 1:2-4 "Hear, O heavens, and give ear, O earth: for the Lord hath spoken, I have nourished and brought up children, and they have rebelled against me. The ox knoweth his owner, and the ass his master's crib: but Israel doth not know, my people doth not consider. Ah sinful nation, a people laden with iniquity, a seed of evildoers, children that are corrupters: they have forsaken the Lord, they have provoked the Holy one of Israel unto anger, they are gone away backward."

The essence of the concept of creation is its ability to identify man as part of God's plan, as part of his own image. Genesis 1:26 "And God said, let us make man in our image, after our likeness: and let them have dominion over the fish of the sea, and over the fowl of the air, and over the cattle, and over all the earth, and over every creeping thing that creepeth upon the earth." When a child sees himself as a creation of God the subsequent logic is that the child will have reason to revere and honour God not only as a creator, but also as the superior being with divine answers to the challenges faced in life by humanity. To the contrary when a child is ignorant of the relevance of God in the life of man, the tendency is that such a child will resort to science and earthly ways when faced with challenges, never believing in the mighty power that is always found in Christ, that way leading to destruction according to the plan of the deceiver, who is the devil himself. That is the whole purpose of strongholds to destroy man.

When one looks at what orphaned or abandoned children go through, it becomes apparent that the lack of a parent figure representing a superior being will many times result in a distorted sense of identity and this in later life destroy the child's self-esteem, pride, confidence and even hope. The fruit of this process is bitterness, rebellion, anger, frustration and hopelessness. The same applies to a child that has been deprived of the knowledge of God. Not knowing God and His plan of salvation leads to frustration, to a life of sin, hatred, rebellion, distress and ultimate destruction, therefore the world is as bad as it is today. People are full of anger, frustration and hatred within and they do not understand why.

When the education system results in people despising God and shunning Christian values, there is need to assess how much the devil has succeeded in manipulating our school systems to move the hearts of man away from their creator. "By giving human wisdom equal weight with biblical revelation Aquinas opened the door for free thinking educators to impart ever more of the wisdom of man even as they discarded the wisdom of God. Eventually man's wisdom has become 'truth' and God's wisdom has become 'error'." Tim Lahaye and David Noebel, *Mind Siege*, page 108. When a man does not know God, the plan of God cannot unfold in his life. He is crippled, paralysed, and this is what the devil wants to happen. He knows well that if a person does not have the knowledge of God he will perish, therefore he is busy feeding people with humanistic knowledge. Hosea 4:6 "My people are destroyed for lack of knowledge: because thou hast rejected knowledge, I will also reject thee, that thou shalt be no priest to me: seeing thou hast forgotten the law of thy God, I will also forget thy children."

The value of an education system in the developed nations cannot be trivialised. However, it is very important that we realise that the nobility of the education system continues to be threatened today by the machinations of the devil, in the name of science. Children are sometimes told to dismiss the doctrine of creation as myth, to dismiss the very existence of God Himself as a mere claim that cannot be proven scientifically, and to look at Christian values as no more than indoctrination that limits people's public liberties. For example, some countries are now considering the inclusion of the need for wives to submit to their husbands during wedding vows to be a breach of women's rights.

It is important for children to know that God is above science, and that He cannot be proven by it because He created it. He begins where science ends, and miracles start where scientific medical treatment ends. The devil establishes strongholds that blinds today's children to the supernatural nature of God. When God has no meaning in the life of today's children, the danger is that future generations will find it more difficult to believe in the power of God, and if unchecked this is the devil's grand plan, to deprive entire generations of the knowledge of God. I am not against education, but I just want you to see how the devil has been so busy throughout influencing world education systems to deprive man of the true knowledge of God.

At school children are taught to prove things, anything that they cannot prove scientifically is not true, therefore God is not true because they cannot prove his existence. Science has become the standard upon which everything is measured against for its authenticity. This is a lie of the devil, life is far more than science. The education system of the world handsomely rewards the mastering of theories that tend to demean the power of God and to exalt the worldly thoughts of men, for example it is highly rewarded to come up with new explanations on Darwin's theory of evolution, perhaps more rewarding than expounding more on the doctrine of creation itself. One tends not to be recognised more explaining the authenticity of the doctrine of creation and promoting the teaching of the word of God on creation is hardly ever rewarded by today's education system. When people spend so many years doing research in universities we are bound to honour them with the respect befitting experts, and when they speak against the doctrine of God, or when they despise God, the tendency is often that they get respected as experts more than they get criticised as heretical and against the teaching of the word of God.

The word of God is not just theory, it applies directly to the lives of people and is used to solve everyday problems and challenges. In fact, the word is alive and can change and transform people's lives from sin to righteousness, bondage to deliverance, sickness to health. Evolutionary theory on the other hand is just a theory in historical analysis but does not apply in making people deal with the problems and challenges in their lives. "A human being whose conscience has been killed is amoral. Consequently, he is capable of performing like the animal he considers himself to be. It is no trouble for him to be inhuman if inhumanity is thought to be an evolutionary advancement." Tim Lahaye and David Noebel, *Mind Siege*, page 144.

Friends
Friends are very important in the formative years of a child. The devil takes advantage of the trust and confidence that one puts in his friends. They trust and believe each other, therefore because of that trust the devil brings humanistic doctrines through the friends and one takes it even if it is against the word of God. Teenage rebellion against parental and societal values is generally centred on friendship, and at this stage trust and confidence is shared more with peers than with adults, especially immediate ones like parents. This time trust has shifted from parents to friends.

The devil establishes strongholds by teaching the child that for example when a child becomes eighteen years, he is now an adult and is now independent, he is now free to do whatever he wants to do. Usually the child becomes rebellious and discipline becomes a major challenge in many of the lives of teenagers. Most of the time the young people preoccupy themselves with this vacuous pride that make them despise all counsel and guidance from the parents, elders, and teachers. Proverbs 16:18 "Pride goeth before destruction, and an haughty spirit before a fall."

When a child is in his teenage period, friends become very important to him and he thinks he knows it all. He thinks his parents are ignorant, they know nothing, and they are backward. He believes almost all things he gets from his friends and wants to experiment with those things. He is doing experiments with life. All this is being engineered by the devil from behind the scenes, and some of the experiments turn out to be very fatal or of permanent harm in life, like trying hard drugs or contracting

HIV and AIDS and some die as a result. These experiments are snares of the devil and they lead to destruction.

The list of trouble and problems that could come one's way through friends are endless, but it is the effects that are worrying. Promising careers are shuttered totally, promising lives are destroyed and visions that could make this world a better place are abruptly terminated or aborted because of disastrous consequences of way ward friendships. It is all happening within the framework of the devil's strongholds, and the grand plan is to destroy the plan of God and to bring suffering in the lives of people. Proverbs 13:20 "He that walketh with wise men shall be wise: but a companion of fools shall be destroyed." Most of the things that are giving people problems today in their lives were planted into their lives when they were young, when they ignorantly received lies through humanistic teachings that oppose the truth of God. They embraced those lies through the machinery that the devil has put in the world without them suspecting anything.

Politicians and Traditional Leaders

Isaiah 9:16 "For the leaders of this people cause them to err; and they that are led of them are destroyed."

Political and traditional leaders are central to the functioning of any society. They help in shaping the beliefs of the people they lead. They have a very big influence over the people they lead. They have the capacity to destroy lives of the people that they lead. When they speak people hear them and people have trust and confidence in them. The devil is quite cognisant of the fact and he manipulates them to promote humanistic doctrines and teachings that are against the word of God. He uses them to promote values, establish laws and pass decrees that are contrary to the word of God. "Traditional leaders are highly respected and influential in their communities. People turn to them for guidance and solutions to different challenges they might face. Even with HIV people have been looking upon us (traditional leaders) and half the time, our interventions were uniformed." Eliezer Wangulu, editor of SAFAIDS, Pretoria South Africa, www.k4health.org.

The leaders are unaware that they are machinery that is being used by the devil to build strongholds in people's minds. They uphold doctrines and traditions that are against the word of God and pass it on from generation to generation. When a child is raised up in a society where the leadership acknowledges and promote idol worship, the natural tendency is to adopt the religion as the truth, and the devil knows that for as long as people worship other gods, the God in heaven will remain unrevealed to them. The devil attaches noble meanings to demonic practices and to some traditional values that in fact run contrary to the word of God. These practices are then honoured and practised by people as part of their culture when in fact they are just infiltrations planted by the devil to achieve his own ends.

Politicians and traditional leaders need to lead people with sober minds and should have the knowledge of the true God of heaven otherwise they will be used by the devil to build strongholds in the lives of the people they lead. "Culture and leadership are probably among the most written about and the least understood topics in the social sciences. This is not only social scientists find these two topics very challenging, even seductive, but also because the two seem necessary for satisfying human existence." *Culture and Leadership Across the World: The GLOBE Book of In-Depth Studies*, Psychology Press, 12/02/2007, page 1.

Cultures and Traditions

Man lives in society with other people and every society has traditions and culture that is unique. All culture and traditions are based on humanistic philosophy and wisdom, and the devil has a lot to do with it. Most of the teachings are contrary to the word of God and have nothing to do with God. Every human being is born in such environments where the norms of those societies are based on lies of the devil, but the people are not aware of it. "A growing number of scholars, journalists, politicians, and development practitioners are focusing on the role of culture values and attitudes as facilitators of, or obstacles to progress." *Culture Matters*, Harrison, Samuel Huntington. Basic Books, 2000, page 21.

This is one of the strongest tools the devil uses to build strongholds. Everybody is what he is because of the culture and tradition that he was born into – you are a product of where you were born. You cannot separate a person from his culture and tradition. This is what is holding back many of us Christians from advancing in the kingdom of God – we still have the mindset of our cultures and traditions. Yes, you love God, but the beliefs and doctrines of your culture are still holding you back. Mark 7:3-9 "For the Pharisees, and all the Jews, except they wash their hands oft, eat not, holding the tradition of the elders. And when they come from the market, except they wash, they eat not. And many other things there be, which they have received to hold, as the washing of cups, and pots, brazen vessels, and tables. Then the Pharisees and Scribes asked Him why not thy disciples according to the tradition of the elders, but eat bread with unwashen hands? He answered and said unto them, well hath Esias prophesied of you hypocrites, as it is written, This people honoureth me with their lips, but their heart is far from me. Howbeit in vain do they worship me, teaching for doctrines the commandments of men. For laying aside the commandment of God, ye hold the tradition men as washing of pots and cups: and many other such like things you do. And he said unto them, Full well ye reject the commandment of God, that ye may keep your own tradition."

Therefore, the word says the minds of children of God must be renewed by the word of God. Many Christians speak the word of God but do not live by that word, but they still live by their cultures and traditions. Once one is born again, he is born into a new life. He is born into the new culture of righteousness and this is his new culture and tradition. The blessings of God are not working in many of us because of the strongholds from our cultures and traditions.

The devil has hidden himself in these cultures and traditions. Colossians 2:8 "Beware lest any man spoil you through philosophy and vain deceit, after the traditions of men, after the rudiments of the world, and not after Christ." 1 Peter 1:18 "Forasmuch as ye know that ye were not redeemed with corruptible things, as silver and gold, from your vain conversation received by tradition from your fathers." This is why Abraham was told by God to leave his father's house, country and relatives. God was telling him to come out of the culture and tradition in which he was born to a new culture of following and being led by God and doing only what God instructed him to do. He was never going to be blessed if he continued in the same environment that he was born with the same old apostate teachings. Genesis 12:1-3 "Now the Lord had said to Abraham get thee out of thy country, and from thy kindred, and from thy father's house, unto a land that I will sew thee: And I will make of thee a great nation, and I will bless thee, and make thy name great; and thou shalt be a blessing: And I will bless them that bless thee, and curse him that curseth thee: and in thee shall all the families of the earth be blessed."

When we come to Christ, we are totally brand-new people who are no longer being led by human culture and traditions. 1 Corinthians 5:17 "Therefore if any man is in Christ, he is a new creature: old things have passed away; behold, all things are become new." Children of God still think, act and see things according to their traditions and culture. Children of God should think, see things and act according to the word of God. 2 Thessalonians 2:15 "Therefore, brethren, stand fast, and hold the traditions which ye have been taught, whether by word or our epistle."

The culture and tradition of God is forgiveness, love, long-suffering, righteousness and holiness etc. Galatians 5:22-25 "But the fruit of the spirit is love, joy, peace, long suffering, gentleness, goodness, faith, meekness, temperance: against such there is no law. And they that are Christ's have crucified the flesh with the affections and lusts. If we live in the Spirit, let us also walk in the Spirit." When every child is born, the devil pollutes his mind through human culture and traditions. Later in life the person finds it very hard to accept the word of God. The satanic, diabolic, devilish wrong teachings that he received whilst young created strongholds that does not allow him to accept the word of God. It was very hard for me to accept the word of God. As I was growing up, I was being taught about ancestral worship and I became a devout worshipper – I did it wholeheartedly, I embraced everything that I saw my elders doing and it only took the grace of God to leave the ancestral worship and then embrace Christ. People are products of their environment, as children of God let us embrace Christ and do away with our cultures and traditions. Colossians 3:9-10 "Lie not one to another, seeing that ye have put off the old man with his deeds; And have put on the new man, which is renewed in knowledge after the image of him that created him."

There is no way children of God can dominate the world if they are controlled by strongholds. Dominion and freedom must start in our minds – there is no freedom if the mind is not free. All suppression and oppression are done in the mind. If one is not living right in his mind his whole life is not well and as a man thinks in his heart so is he – no man can live above what he thinks. The mind is central, it is where everything about man is processed. Political freedom is not true freedom, the same people who have political freedom without the freedom of the mind will after gaining the so-called freedom can start to fight again among themselves, oppress and kill each other. Therefore, there is no genuine freedom outside of Christ. John 8:36 "If the son therefore shall make you free, ye shall be free indeed."

Religion
The power of doctrine cannot be underestimated in shaping the behaviour and character of young people. Religion is the most effective way of indoctrinating people. Matthew 23:15 "Woe to you, scribes and Pharisees, hypocrites! For you travel land and sea to win one proselyte, and when he is won, you make him twice as much a son of hell as yourselves." Through religion, people can become adamantly dogmatic and fanatical about doctrines that run contrary to the true doctrine of Christ. Most of the time these satanic doctrines are centred on cult religious heroes who are believed to be powerful that every person is expected to revere and believe what they stand for, and of course they stand for heresies and lies of the devil. Their word is final and not the true word of God.

When Jesus came preaching about the kingdom of God, he faced greater opposition from religious leaders not from people of the world. The Pharisees and the Sadducees believed they were practising true worship of God, and the devil had over time deceived these religious leaders into practicing hypocrisy, doing all things to be glorified by man and never to please God, paying lip service to the teachings of the word of God and to the law of Moses. So confused and misled were the Pharisees and Sadducees that they were greatly angered by the teachings of Jesus Christ. They began to plot His death. John 11:47-49 "Then gathered the chief priests and the Pharisees a council, and said, what do we? For this man doeth many miracles. If we let him thus alone, all men will believe on him: and the Romans shall come and take away both our place and nation. And one of them, named Caiaphas, being the high priest that same year, said unto them, Ye know nothing at all, Nor consider that it is expedient for us, that one man should die for the people, and that the whole nation perish not."

Religious deception comes in many ways, from hypocrites that lead double standard lives, to those who interpret scriptures in devious ways to suit the plans of the devil. They do all this unknowingly, the devil uses them. There are many people who deny Christ today because of certain religious values instilled in them by religious leaders when they were growing up. So many have been abused by church leaders, people whom they respected and honoured, people whom they thought were men and women of God. The way I grew up was a typical deception, I grew up being taught things that I thought were the ways of God, yet they were not. I embraced everything only to discover later that this was not the true doctrine of Christ. It was only by the grace of God that Christ found me. The wrong teachings about Jesus that was in me made me to reject the truth about him when I heard it. Strongholds Cause you to reject and to doubt about the existence of God.

True Christianity is authored by Jesus Christ Himself, and as a counterfeit to Christianity the devil has authored religion. Religion seeks to make people ritualistic, and it is merely a form of worship designed by the devil to keep people in the delusion that they are worshipping God. It was religion that stood in greatest opposition to the ministry of Jesus Christ. It was religious leaders that schemed the crucifixion of Jesus Christ. Religion can lead people into violent conduct and when they kill for religion, they are often convinced that they will be acting in God's service or even defence. John 9: 1-2 "And Saul yet breathing out threatenings and slaughter against the disciples of the Lord, went unto the high priest, and desired of him letters to Damascus to the synagogues, that if he found any of this way, whether they were men or women, he might bring them bound to Jerusalem."

Often religious people have understanding about scriptures from the academic point of view, they do not understand scriptures spiritually and there is no personal relationship between the believer and God. There is a relationship more with the doctrinal teachings than there is with God Himself. Practicing religious people do not show fruits of repentance. Titus 1:16 "They profess that they know God; but in works they deny Him, being abominable, and disobedient, and unto every good work reprobate."

God is not interested in religion because religion is the best enemy of God. God is tremendously interested in giving people life, this is why in the New Testament Jesus did not hesitate to break the Sabbath regulations of His day when those regulations violated the real need of a broken human being for healing. God is not no interest in the beautiful stained- glass cathedral windows, organ music, congregational hymns, or some ritual kind of prayers as He is in the business of producing love-filled homes, generous hearts, and brave men and women who can live godly lives in the midst of all adversity in this evil world. His goal for our lives is that we be people of sober and undefiled minds and undefiled hearts, living and projecting His truth and His character in a sin ridden world. Religion on the other hand is based on the power of the law and as such it cannot change the inside man. It seeks and teaches human philosophy mixed with the word of God. All is done by the devil to build strongholds. Isaiah 29:13 "Wherefore the Lord said forasmuch as this people draw near me with their mouth, and with their lips do honour me, but have removed their heart far from me, and their fear toward me is taught by the precepts of men."

Today the preaching of Jesus Christ is frowned upon and despised by many people because they hold on to one form of counterfeit religion or another. As a young man growing up with the zeal to worship and to serve God I got enrolled into a higher religious institute of learning. The things that I started to see the leaders doing and what they were teaching destroyed all my love and zeal to continue serving God. I thank God who found me at the verge of perishing and saved me. A very big stronghold had been built in me that caused me to think that there was no God in heaven. One day I spoke to one of the lecturers asking to get more understanding about hell and heaven. The answer that I got shocked and devastated me. The lecturer said that it was a risk believing in either of the two, he said no one is sure if heaven and hell really existed, it's just a myth. I regretted why I was wasting time trying to serve God who does not exist. The following day my friend and I left the institute and we went wild and started to live in sin. We went flat out sinning because someone had told us that hell and heaven was just a myth therefore God was not there everything was a myth.

Wrong teachings, heresies, that are taught in religious circles cause many people to stop loving God, he is presented in a frustrating, complicated way, and in the end you get confused and do not want to hear or have anything to do with God again. Throughout the world and ages, we have heard about some religious leaders who sexually abuse children. The children trusted them as men and women of God and they were supposed to be examples to the children – the children were supposed to see God through them. Now imagine the damage that is caused when the child is abused by such a person. The child will never love God again unless the hand of God comes upon that child. He will be rebellious to anything that has to do with God. Such leaders are used by demons to build big stronghold in the lives of the children. Many people do not love God today because of some horrible ordeals they went through in some religious circles.

Media
The power of media in building strongholds in people's lives cannot be underestimated. Today's main opinion shapers include the internet, television, radio, magazines, newspapers, Facebook etc. People are often as gullible as to believe that anything that the media print is fact and truth – most people believe whatever is screened on television has substance. They are not aware that the devil is behind the scenes controlling everything happening. Even Hollywood movies have become major character shapers, altering lifestyles and changing cultures across the world. Many young people of today even many adults will site film actors as their role models despite the personality they so wish to live is just an acted script and not reality. The devil is doing all this to pollute the minds of the people.

The media manufactures a certain behaviour that is contrary to reality or to the will of God. By merely side-lining Christianity and not promoting happenings in the Christian community the devil through the media has managed to create in many people the notion that Christianity is a triviality they can afford to live without. When the media covers something about Christianity often it is scandals and negative stories that are picked up to demean the spreading of the Gospel of Jesus Christ. There is nothing wrong about reporting scandals or any other negative story. However, when the media selectively reports on the negatives, turning a blind eye and deaf ear on all the great things God is doing, then it is a horrible conspiracy concocted straight from the depths of hell.

All the media creates is a world of wars, earthquakes, disease, hunger, famines, and oppressions. This leads people into hopelessness that can cause depression and great melancholy across nations. When the media creates strongholds like the strongholds of fear the implications are quite tremendous. A world of fear-filled people has no hope and can hardly ever progress. More than three hundred times the phrase "fear not" appears in the bible, and this is precisely because God knows that nothing can be accomplished with fear. The devil is using the media to create so much fear in the people. We fear terrorists, wars, diseases and all sorts of trouble that are magnified as insurmountable through the media. The fear of Covid 19 has caused the whole world to come to a standstill. Our politics, economies and even our faith is altered and shaped by the media. Hopelessness, sadness and despair are all strongholds created by the media, so it becomes easier for the devil to control and manipulate people in the whole world. He is managing very well because people are not aware of his presence in the media and the happenings.

There is nothing inherently wrong with the media as a necessity in society, but media power that constructs and builds is what God prefers. The media, if it were not under the influence of the devil, would certainly do a better job by highlighting more hope in Christianity, and the hope that is in the salvation that comes through believing in Jesus Christ.

Media censorship is done by people who are fully aware of the power of media, therefore films are age rated and so on. Many serial killers have been found to be victims of films they watched as they grew up – admirers of evil who instead of finding murder deplorable, they develop a yearning to kill endlessly – that is what the media can do. The media shapes fashion and taste, and many young people of today dress the way they do because of what they have watched on television or seen in a magazine, movie etc. Television culture creates a superficial people that is very easy to manipulate and control and that is the whole purpose of the devil.

Sexual immorality, ranging from fornication, masturbation, rape, homosexuality, seduction, pornography, incest to prostitution and bestiality has been a product of the television and the internet. Before the television and the internet these were being done privately but today, they are a public feature, and that was the goal of the devil. Young men are enslaved in this perversion and it is very difficult to get them out of the addiction – and many have grown into adulthood as slaves of all sorts of fantasies of sexual immorality. Therefore the marriage institution is now threatened so severely – with so many divorces and infidelity going on. The devil has used the media so strongly in attacking God's people with the stronghold of sexual immorality.

Pornography has been used by the devil to expose children to the demon of sexual perversion, and the idea is to catch them when they are still young so that they are so weak to get out of it when they get older. Now more and more countries are beginning to legalise homosexuality and prostitution, we have sex workers it is considered a job. It is the devil creating a stronghold in the minds of the people to normalise sin and making sin part of the people's way of living. People are led by the wickedness of their hearts – they have developed a whole industry of pornography which is generating billions and billions of dollars every day. The young and the old watch the pornographic films without feeling guilty and everything has become normal. As they watch these films without them realising strongholds of sexual immorality are formed in their minds, sooner or later they find they cannot think of anything else except sex. School children cannot concentrate in class – their minds are always hooked to sex. Adults on the other hand cannot perform well at work their minds are full of the movies they were watching, and their marriages are affected at the same time. They cannot get satisfied by their own wives or husbands sexually because they have in their minds the porn stars.

The biggest part of the internet pages contain pornography, which is causing so much damage to society. If these people could only realize how much damage and evil, they bring to themselves and into the lives of those who watch their product they would not have done it. They will never realize because they are slaves of the devil and he does not give them the chance to come to their senses.

CHAPTER 3

TYPES OF STRONGHOLDS

The Stronghold of Fear
After seeing how strongholds are built and some weapons that are used, we are now going to see some strongholds. There are so many, but we are going to see a few of them. We can start with the stronghold of fear.

God does not want his children to live in fear – faith cannot function where there is fear. Therefore, the devil brings fear into the people of God because he wants to remove faith from them. Hebrews 11:6 "But without faith it is impossible to please Him: for he that cometh to God must believe that he is, and he is a rewarder of them that diligently seek him."

Several times in the word of God, God emphasises the fact that His children should not fear. Isaiah 41:10 "Fear thou not, for I am with thee: be not dismayed; for I am thy God: I will strengthen thee; yea, I will help thee, yea, I will uphold thee with the right hand of my righteousness." Joshua 1:9 "Have not I commanded thee? Be strong and of a good courage; be not afraid, neither be thou dismayed: for the Lord thy God is with thee withersover thou goest."

Fear is an emotional state which overcomes a man when he faces situations that surpasses his capacity and ability to manage or handle. In this state he might see death staring at him, or he sees himself losing things that he values so much, things which he thinks he cannot do without, things which he thinks adds value and respect to his life. When those things are seriously threatened or when his life is threatened fear attacks him, fear gets hold of him.

When God created man, He never created him to be independent. He made him to depend on Him, if he tries to live alone, fear overwhelms him whether he likes it or not. The devil knows that man cannot successfully live without God, he influences him to want to live independently. He teaches him things that are contrary to the word of God, and the gospel of the devil is to teach man to do it alone.

The number one need for man is security – if that security is threatened fear comes upon him. The devil does not want man to know that his security is in God – instead he teaches him that his security is in money, houses, investments, other people, parents, husbands, wives, friends even children. These things and people cannot give permanent security they are all temporary.

The devil influences man to have faith and believe in material things, that can be there today and tomorrow they are not. The devil can control the material things that is why he wants people to have faith in those things. When he takes away the houses and the money then he can paralyse and even kill the victim with fear. He can steal the peace and the joy of people by playing around with the material things. He does not want people to put their trust in God who is permanent. Job who trusted in God, when all his wealthy was destroyed and his children, because he had all his trust in God he was never moved. Job 1:21 "And said naked came I out of my mother's womb, and naked shall I return thither: The Lord hath taken away; blessed be the name of the Lord."

Fear is the biggest weapon of the devil – fear can make a man die so many times before his real death. The devil takes away peace and joy from people through fear of the unknown, fear of the future. Most of the things that people fear many times they do not encounter them. Fear may bring anxiety, diverse kinds of sicknesses, for example heart attacks, high blood pressure, kidney disease etc. Having the knowledge of the word of God and having full knowledge of who God casts away all fear. 1 John 4:18 "There is no fear in love; but perfect love casteth out fear: because fear hath torment. He that feareth is not made perfect in love." Man, without God is empty and as a result he is full of fear – he does not know why he is afraid, but he is full of fear every day of his life. Proverbs 28:1 "The wicked flee when no man pursueth: but the righteous are bold as a lion."

People suffer from fear, it is not only people who do not know God even those who know God. That stronghold of fear that was built in people's lives before they knew God and usually continues with them even when they are children of God unless they destroy it. There are people in church who are full of fear, and this is the reason for this book so that strongholds can be destroyed. Strongholds do not just get destroyed automatically when you come to Christ – you must know them and it is your job to destroy them, not God. Many Christians are being troubled by the strongholds which have not been destroyed.

Fear is a big problem, those not married especially ladies are afraid, not sure if they shall find someone who will marry them. Some are afraid of becoming sick and the fear of death. Fear of the unknown, fear of failure. Fear affects the rich and the poor alike. The rich man is afraid of bankruptcy and the poor man is afraid of dying poor. Many times, man tries to cover up his fear by taking alcohol, sex, violence, buying expensive clothes, buying nice houses, expensive cars, travelling to different parts of the world etc. Through fear the devil has ability to manipulate people.

Fear of death is another deadly stronghold. Daniel 3:16-18 "Shadrach, Meshach and Abednego, answered and said to the king, O Nebuchadnezzar, we are not careful to answer thee in this matter. If it be so our God whom we serve is able to deliver us from out of thine hand, O king, that we will not serve thy gods, nor worship the golden image which thou hath set up." These had no fear of death at all they fully trusted their God. If children of God are afraid of death, we cannot overcome the devil and manifest the kingdom of God in our generation. The prophets and the apostles in the word of God did exploits during their time because they did not have the stronghold of fear of death. They could face furnaces of fire and get into dens of lions without fear whatsoever – all the heroes of faith overcame the stronghold of fear.

Generally, every human being is afraid of death – it is a subject which people do not want to talk about, even in churches. It is not preached about, yet it is an experience that no one is going to escape from. Let me try to explain in short what death does to a child of God. Death transfers us from the natural world into the supernatural world of God which is a better world. It brings us face to face with the heavenly Father. This is why Paul said for him to die was gain. Philippians 1:21 "For me to live is Christ, and to die is gain." Paul had no fear of death – he was looking forward to dying so that he could be with the Lord. Death transfers us into eternity, it relieves us from all the pain and hardships that we go through in this life.

People who do not know God should have the reasons to fear death but not children of God. Children of God fear death because they lack the knowledge of who God is. We sing about wanting to go and be with the Lord but at the same time we do not want to die. We seem in some of our songs as if the only desire that we have is to go and be with the Lord. If children of God are afraid of death the devil is going to continue to use it to afflict them. When the worst comes to the worst, when he wants them to disown their God, he always threatens them with death. It is the last and biggest weapon that he uses to pressurise people into submission to his will. If a man is free from the stronghold of fear the devil loses power over him. Shadrach, Meshack and Abednego demonstrated this truth in the word of God. Daniel 3:16-18 "Shadrach, Meshach, and Abednego, answered and said to the king, O Nebuchadnezzar, we are not careful to answer thee in this matter. If it be so, our God whom we serve is able to deliver us from the burning fiery furnace, and he will deliver us out of thine hand, O king. But if not, be it known unto thee, O king, that we will not serve thy gods, nor worship the golden image which thou hath set up." We are children of God, but we do not want to go to our Father. A child would not cry when he is told you are going to your father tomorrow whom he has not seen for a long time. He will rejoice but children of God are afraid to go and meet with their Father God. It shows that we do not understand what we are doing, we do not understand much about the God that we profess to worship.

The Stronghold of Sickness
The devil has taught the world through his lies so well that sickness has been well accepted as something very normal that must happen to every human being. According to the word of God sickness is a curse. Deuteronomy 28:20-22 "The Lord shall send upon thee cursing, vexation, and rebuke, in all that thou settest thine hand unto for to do, until thou be destroyed, and until thou perish; because of the wickedness of thy doings, whereby thou hast forsaken me. The Lord shall make the pestilence cleave unto thee, until he have consumed thee from off

the land, whither thou goest to possess it. The Lord shall smite thee with a consumption, and with fever, and with an inflammation, and with an extreme burning, and with the sword, and with blasting, and with mildew; and they shall pursue thee until thou perish." People are afflicted by terrible pain through sickness, many believe that sickness comes from God. How can God bring sickness and at the same time provide healing through the power of the Holy Spirit? Mark 16:17-18 "And these signs shall follow them that believe; In my name shall they cast out devils; they shall speak with new tongues. They shall take up serpents; it shall not hurt them; they shall lay hands on the sick, and they shall recover." Isaiah 53:4-5 "Surely he hath borne our griefs and carried our sorrows: yet we did esteem him stricken, smitten of God, and afflicted. But he was wounded for our transgressions, he was bruised for our iniquities: the chastisement of our peace was upon him; and with his stripes we are healed."

The devil has managed to cause people to believe that sickness comes from God and not from him – there is confusion in the hearts of man. They say if God is that good why does he allow diseases to play havoc on the innocent, the young and the old. He has managed to shift all the blame from himself to God. He is a liar, he has managed to change his lies into truth. Romans 1:25 "Who changed the truth of God into a lie and worshipped and served the creature more than the creator, who is blessed for ever. Amen."

The source of all sickness is the devil. Jesus came to give us health that was taken by the devil. John 10:10 "The thief cometh not, but for to steal, and to kill, and to destroy: I am come that they might have life, and that they might have it more abundantly." The thief is the devil who steals your health. When he does that, he does not want you to know because he is a thief. Thieves do steal under cover of darkness, they do not want to be known or caught. The devil is the prince of darkness. Jesus came to stop every work of the devil. 1 John 3:8 "He that committeth sin is of the devil; for the devil sinneth from the beginning. For this purpose, the son of God was manifested, that he might destroy the works of the devil." Afflicting people with sickness is one of his works.

Sickness is a curse and the author of curses is the devil. God does not want His children to be sick that is why from the beginning he was protecting his people against sickness, even in Egypt he protected the children of Israel. Deuteronomy 7:15 "And the Lord will take away from thee all sickness, and will put none of the evil diseases of Egypt, which thou knowest, upon thee; but will lay them upon all them that hate thee."

Man was created to live a healthy life – he got sick by his own choice, when he disobeyed God. One of the consequences of disobeying God is sickness. When man made the choice, he was ignorant of the consequences. Through Adam, man became sick but through Christ man is made healthy. Sickness is not the plan of God upon man, man is sick because he believed the lies of the devil. Children of God are sick because they do not have faith in God – they do not believe the word of God. You do not automatically get healed because you have received Christ. You must appropriate your healing through faith by the word of God – if you do not you will continue to be sick. That is not God's problem it is your problem – if you do what you are supposed to do according to the word of God, you will stop sickness from afflicting you.

Ignorance of the word of God is what is making many children of God suffer from sickness. Galatians 3:13 "Christ hath redeemed us from the curse of the law, being made a curse for us: for it is written, cursed is everyone that hangeth on a tree." We were redeemed from sickness. Matthew 8:17 "That it might be fulfilled which was spoken by Esaias the prophet, saying, Himself took our infirmities, and bare our sickness." 1 Peter 2:24 "Who His own self bare our sins in his own body on the tree, that we, being dead to sins, should live unto righteousness: by whose stripes ye were healed."

People need the healing of the mind more than the healing of their bodies. If a man does not think right the result is sickness of the body. What is to think right? To think right is to think in line with the word of God, thinking against the word of God affects the mind. The lies of the devil are like a virus in a computer. When a computer is hit by a virus it stops functioning the way it was designed to function. It is the same with the lies of the devil in a man's mind – when those lies hit the mind, a person ceases to function the way God designed him to function, and this may result in sickness.

The way people think has been programmed by the devil through traditions and cultures of the world. This is done secretly by the devil without anyone suspecting that there is something bad that is happening. The devil and his demons are working very hard behind the scenes for people to see things in the way he wants them to see and understand. He is giving people a wrong perspective of how they must see the world and life at large. The minds of people are constantly fed with jealousy, hatred, vengeance, violence, greedy, etc. All these are strongholds that produce negative effects in a person. These things may produce sickness in man if left unmanned for a long period of time.

Our Lord Jesus Christ never got sick because He always thought right – not one stronghold was built in His mind. Wrong thinking can suffocate the body and as a result one gets sick. The body cannot handle the load transmitted to it by the mind which is full of negative thoughts. Our bodies cannot handle negative words. Proverbs 3:7-8 "Be not wise in thine own eyes: fear the Lord and depart from evil. It shall be health to thy naval, and marrow to thy bones." Proverbs 15:30 "The light of the eyes rejoice the heart: and a good report maketh the bones fat." Proverbs 17:22 "A merry heart doeth good like a medicine: but a broken spirit drieth the bones."

The stronghold of sickness works together with the stronghold of death. When one is sick the devil is always reminding the sick person that he is going to die, and the man dies several times before his death. The devil does that so that the man can accept death. He knows that as a man thinks in his heart so is he, if one continues to think about death he will eventually die. Everything starts in the mind, the mind is very powerful. What continues to run in your mind that is what you will become. As one continues to think about death all hope is stolen, joy, peace and faith. The person becomes miserable and surrenders and waits for fate to take its course.

The devil is on a distraction rampage, he has gone even into food that we eat. Through the so-called technology we are now eating genetic modified foods all over the world, he has taken away all organic food from the market. People are eating junk food and the result is diseases and sickness. Most of the diseases that people suffer from today come because of the wrong food that people are exposed to. He has destroyed the soil from where we should get organic food by introducing fertilizers and many chemicals in the name of technology and advancement, that are being used in farming today. The chemicals have corrupted the soil, the soil no longer has the energy to produce crops without the chemicals. The foods that we eat are full of chemicals and that is what we are feeding on, the result is so many cancerous diseases in the world today.

The Stronghold of Sexual Immorality

Sexual immorality has been normalised. Why? People have identified themselves with animals. They do not understand who they are and where they came from and have believed the lies of the devil through some satanic doctrines and now believe that they evolved from a chimpanzee. Animals have sex with their offspring even their mothers. Man is also sleeping with his mother, sister etc. In some circles, brothers and sisters are having sex with each other – they do not see anything wrong with it.

Man has lost self-respect and value; homosexuality is being accepted as a norm in many countries of the world today. When it comes to homosexuality, man has degenerated even more than an animal. I grew up seeing animals, but I never saw animals of the same sex having sex with each other. Animals have become smarter than human beings; man, who is supposed to be rational, has become so base that he cries to get the liberty to have sex with another man, and a woman with another woman. This is now being taught everywhere even in schools that it is normal. Our children are taught by some of these people who think that this is very normal. What are they teaching our children? Humanistic teachings say that homosexuality is a decision rather than an inherited trait. They say it's not perversion, and it's not demon possession. However, the word of God clearly shows that this is perversion. Romans 1:24-32 "Wherefore God also gave them up to uncleanness through the lusts of their own hearts, to dishonour their own bodies between themselves: Who changed the truth of God into a lie, and worshipped and served the creature more than the creator, who is blessed for ever. Amen. For this cause God gave up unto vile affections: for even their women did change the natural use into that which is against nature: And likewise also the men, leaving the natural use of the woman, burned in their lust one

toward another; men with men working that which is unseemly, and receiving in themselves that recompence of their error which was meet. And even as they did not like to retain God in their knowledge, God gave them over to a reprobate mind, to do those things which are not convenient; Being filled with all unrighteousness, fornication, wickedness, covetousness, maliciousness; full of envy, murder, debate, deceit, malignity; whisperers, Back biters, haters of God, despiteful, proud, boasters, inventors of evil things, disobedient to parents, Without understanding, covenant-breakers, without natural affection, implacable, unmerciful: Who knowing the judgement of God, that they which commit such things are worthy of death, not only do the same, but have pleasure in them that do them."
"The truth is amorality does not provide a happy, fulfilling life. Its hallmarks are disease, discouragement, and death." Tim Lahaye and David Noebel, *Mind Siege*, page 145.

Sexual immorality is being taken as part of the culture of the world – most people are very ignorant of the fact that sexual immorality is perversion. They think it's normal, they were born into it and grew up in it – they were born in iniquity and grew up in iniquity. Psalm 51:5 "Behold I was shapen in iniquity, and in sin did my mother conceive me."

The Stronghold of Poverty
The source of wealth is God not the company that one is working for or the business someone is doing. The devil has told people so many lies, for example that unless someone has a university degree there is no way one can have financial prosperity, he will die poor. The person starts to live a hopeless life, because he is bound by his belief.

My financial prosperity and my source are God not my company or university degree. Companies do not give me money that is enough to make me a wealthy person. They pay people enough money to buy food and pay rent so that they continue to go to work the next day. Proverbs 10:22 "The blessing of the Lord, maketh rich, and addeth no sorrow with it." Jesus Christ came to the world to deliver me and you from poverty. 2 Corinthians 8:9 "For ye know the grace of our Lord Jesus Christ, that, though he was rich, yet for your sakes he became poor, that ye through is poverty might be rich." Jesus came so that I may have life in abundance. John 10:10 "The thief cometh not, but for to steal, and to kill, and to destroy: I am come that they might have life, and that they have it more abundantly."

Many children of God are poor because they have not put their eyes to God, but they have put their eyes upon their salaries, and they are limited by their salaries and wages. They have faith in their salaries and not upon God. Since salaries are not enough, living in debt has been accepted as a norm. The bible says children of God shall not borrow but they should lend to nations. Deuteronomy 15:6 "For the Lord thy God blesseth thee, as he promised thee: and thou shalt lend unto many nations, but thou shalt not borrow; and thou shalt reign over many nations, but they shall not reign over thee." The bible also says the borrower is a slave to the lender. Proverbs 22:7 "The rich ruleth over the poor, and the borrower is servant to the lender." The eyes of man have been directed to the banks and other lending institutions. Some Christians borrow from banks and they think that God has blessed them. God does not bless his people by enslaving them, it is only the devil who enslaves people. The banks and lending institutions do not use the principles of God, they use the Babylonian system, satanic, diabolic system. These lending institutions are controlled by the devil who is the prince of this world.

When the bank gives you money to buy a house that house

is not yours until you finish paying for it. The interests that you pay are so high, it is like you are buying two or more houses, and you are bound for life paying the mortgage. Many die and leave the loan for the children to inherit. Many Christians think that God has blessed them when they get a loan from the bank, that is the lie of the devil. When you are given money by the bank that is not a blessing from God – you are not blessed, you have become poorer than what you were before you got the money. Before getting the money, you were a free man but once you got the money you become bound, you are now a slave to the bank until the day you pay the last cent.

The devil has built a very big stronghold in the minds of the people even businesspeople. Many businesspeople believe that it is impossible to run a business without going into debt. I have seen people die because of debts. I have also seen people developing complicated diseases because of debts, and once happy marriages crumbling down because of debts. Some Christians fast and pray so that they may be given loans from the bank. That is a wrong kind of prayer, it is against the will of God and if you get that prayer answered it is not God but the devil.

I was delivered from the stronghold of debt by my spiritual father, Professor Ezekiel Guti. I was in debt from every angle of my life when I came to the Lord and I thought it was normal. The clothes that I was wearing, food, house, car, all the furniture, they were bought on credit. When he taught about debt I got delivered, I started to hate debt from the depth of my heart. I got delivered but this did take away the debts, I had to pay back the people that I owed money. I started to work very hard and fought very hard to raise money to finish off all the debts. This was not easy; it took me some years to finish the payments. I had to sell the house that I had bought on debt and paid back the bank its money.

After paying back all the monies that I owed I was left with nothing except God. However, I then put my focus on God and started to believe what the word of God says and how God blesses His children. I continued seeking the face of God and God started to bless me step by step, it was not easy I had to fight the fight of faith and today I have houses, not one, but many houses which I built on cash, no mortgage. I did not borrow any money, neither did I steal any money, but God gave me the money because He is true and faithful – I have seen Him doing things in my life.

If we want to see the hand of God in our lives, we cannot see it if we use the Babylonian system. The kingdom of God has its own system and principles. Governments of the world have been locked up in this debt stronghold, they think they cannot improve the lives of their people without getting into debt with the World Bank and the International Monetary Fund. They cannot believe in God to give them money to run their countries. If the World Bank gives a country money that country is no longer free, the bank starts to control the country. Before the bank releases the money, the country must comply with their demands. They tell the country how big their civil service should be before they release the money and the country must comply.

Nations are in trouble because they have put their eyes to human institutions for help instead of believing God. IMF, World bank have taken the place of God especially to some third world countries. If they do not get money from the World Bank, then the sufferings of their people are justified. The devil is controlling the fate of nations and individuals through the stronghold of debt. With God all developing nations can develop to all levels they want to reach, but if their eyes are upon these institutions, they shall stay poor for ever. They also need to change their name of being called third world – God never created a third world that is another lie of the devil. God created the world and He saw that it was good. When you put yourself in a certain class which is considered low then you start to see yourself as someone who is low and eventually you will become low. Proverbs 23:7 "For as he thinketh in his heart, so is he: Eat and drink, saith he to thee; but his heart is not with thee."

CHAPTER 4

HOW ARE STRONGHOLDS DESTROYED?

Demons are not always present in a person, but strongholds are built in a man and are always present in him. As I said earlier on strongholds have power to paralyse a man's life. Demons can be cast out and go but strongholds will not be destroyed when demons go, they remain. They are like structures built in the mind of a man and are hard to destroy.

Many Christians think that their problems are caused by demons but, I have seen that most of man's problems come because of strongholds. Strongholds are built by demons and demons are attracted by strongholds. Therefore, it is important when demons are cast out, the person must change his way of thinking and of doing things. If one continues with the same mindset demons that have been cast will come and possess him again. Matthew 12:43-45 "When the unclean spirit is gone out of a man, he walketh through dry places, seeking rest, and findeth none. Then he saith, I will return into my house from whence I came out; and when he is come, he findeth it empty, swept and garnished. Then goeth he, and taketh with himself seven other spirits more wicked than himself, and they enter in and dwell there: and the last state of that man is worse than the first. Even so shall it be also unto this wicked generation." It takes more than just going to church to destroy strongholds. There are many people in church who are still being oppressed by strongholds.

The following are powerful spiritual weapons that God has given us children of God to use to destroy strongholds. It is not God who does the work of destroying strongholds. It is you and me who must do the work using weapons that he has provided. God did everything He was supposed to do at Calvary. John 19:30 When Jesus therefore had received the vinegar, he said, it is finished: and he bowed his head, and gave up the ghost. God has done everything it takes for us to get our freedom from the devil but there are some things that we have to do in order for us to enjoy what he did for us. If you do not use the weapons, then there is nothing that will change in your life. It would appear as if Jesus did nothing. He gave us the power to do all that we must do. John 1:12 "But as many as received him, to them gave he power to become the sons of God, even to them that believe on his name." The weapons that God has given us are, the word of God, faith, the Holy Spirit, prayer and fasting, the blood of Jesus Christ, ministerial gifts (that is, the fivefold gifts) and the name of Jesus Christ. We are going to see briefly how the weapons work and how we can destroy strongholds.

The Word of God
You can only counteract the lies or the deception of the devil by the word of God. You cast down every thought that comes into your mind that opposes the word of God by the word of God. Feed your mind with the word of God, that run contrary to what the devil and his demons has been feeding you with. Meditate on the word of God until that word becomes part of you and create a new thinking pattern, a new mindset. If one continues to meditate on things that are contrary to the word of God, you are feeding the strongholds and they become stronger. When you meditate on the word of God you weaken them and as a result they crumble, and they are destroyed.

The word of God has two major purposes – to give us the nature of God and to pull down strongholds. Ephesians 4:21-25 "If so be that ye have heard him, and have been taught by him, as the truth is in Jesus: That ye put off concerning the former conversation the old man, which is corrupt according to the deceitful lusts; And be renewed in the spirit of your mind; and that ye put on the new man, which after God is created in righteousness and true holiness. Wherefore putting away lying, speak every man truth with his neighbour: for we are members one of another." 2 Corinthians 10:4-5 "For the weapons of our warfare are not canal, but mighty through God to the pulling down of strongholds; Casting down imaginations, and every high thing that exalteth itself against the knowledge of God, and bringing into captivity every thought to the obedience of Christ."

Every teaching that is received as one is growing up, that is contrary to the word of God creates strongholds. It is by taking the word of God that strongholds are destroyed. Joshua 1:8 "This book of the law shall not depart out of thy mouth; but thou shalt meditate therein day and night, that thou mayest observe to do according to all that is written therein: for then thou shalt make thy way prosperous, and then thou shalt have good success." Strongholds are spiritual, they can only be destroyed by the word of God which is spiritual. John 6:63 "It is the spirit that quickeneth; the flesh profiteth nothing: the words that I speak unto you, they are spirit, and they are life."

The word of God that is only in your mind is not able to destroy strongholds – it is the word that gets into your spirit. The word of God is seed that must be planted in your spirit, and it only becomes effective when it is coming out of my spirit as I declare it through the power of the Holy Spirit. Proverbs 4:20-23 "My son, attend to my words; incline thine ear unto my sayings. Let them not depart from thine eyes; keep them in the midst of thine heart. For they are life unto those that find them, and health to all their flesh. Keep thy heart with all diligence; for out of it are the issues of life." Psalm 1:1-3 "Blessed is the man that walketh not in the counsel of the ungodly. Nor standeth in the way of sinners, nor sitteth in the seat of the scornful. But his delight is in the law of the Lord; and in his law doth he meditate day and night. And he shall be like a tree planted by the rivers of water, that bringeth forth his fruit in his season, his leaf also shall not wither; and whatsoever he doeth shall prosper."

The word of God that is spoken from the mind does not have the power to transform your life and it cannot destroy strongholds. The word that has power to transform and destroy strongholds is the word of God spoken from the spirit man. Speak the word of God from your spirit. Job 22:28 "Thou shalt also decree a thing, and it shall be established unto thee: and the light shall shine upon thy ways." Your spirit is the spirit of God, it is the part that was put into man by God. Genesis 2:7 "Then the Lord God formed man from the dust of the ground and breathed into his nostrils the breath of life, and the man became a living being." When the word of God gets into your spirit faith is born, and it has the power to destroy strongholds in your life. Faith disperses all fear, and faith cannot be stopped by anything, even strongholds.

Your life is in your spirit, God hid your life in your spirit. When you feed your spirit with the word of God, life is activated. Out of your spirit are the issues of life. Strongholds destroy all the life that has been put in you by God in your spirit. Proverbs 4:23 "Keep thy heart with all diligence; for out of it are the issues of life."

The word of God is spirit therefore, it must be understood

spiritually, if we are to get results of what it says. For it to destroy strongholds it must be understood spiritually. John 6:63 "It is the spirit that quikeneth; the flesh profiteth nothing; the words that I speak unto you, they are spirit, and they are life." 1 Corinthians 2:14 "But the natural man receiveth not the things of the spirit of God: for they are foolishness unto him: neither can he know them, because they are spiritually discerned." The devil is not worried if people do all other things but neglect the word of God. Whatever is done in the name of the Lord but ignoring the word has nothing to do with God and it does not please God. No man can be set free from strongholds if he does not take the word of God seriously. Religion does all other things but does not take the word of God seriously. The author of religion is the devil and his demons. Many children of God today are busy working for God but they are doing very little with the word of God. The spirit of God cannot work in us effectively unless we are full of the word in our spirits. Colossians 3:16 "Let the word of Christ dwell in you richly in all wisdom; teaching and admonishing one another in psalms and hymns and spiritual songs, singing with grace in your hearts to the Lord."

Strongholds are destroyed as we study the word of God spiritually, as we meditate upon the word. Proverbs 1:8 "This book of the law shall not depart out of thy mouth; but thou shalt meditate therein day and night, that thou mayest observe to do according to all that is written: for then thou shalt make thy way prosperous, and then thou shalt have good success." Psalm 119:7-10 "O how love I thy law! It is my meditation all day. Thou through thy commandments hast made me wiser than mine enemies: for they are ever with me. I have more understanding than all my teachers: for thy testimonies are my meditation. I understand more than the ancients, because I keep thy precepts."

Psalm 119:130 "The entrance of thy words giveth; light it giveth understanding unto the simple." The understanding that one gets from the truth of the word of God destroys every stronghold. The understanding of all that is contrary to the word of God build strongholds.

Let us look at meditation – what is it, and how do we it? Meditation is deep profound thinking about what God says through His word. It is being in class with the Holy Spirit, receiving revelations and getting spiritual understanding of the scriptures. It is fellowship with the Holy Spirit allowing Him to drill into your spirit certain hidden truths from the word of God. Meditation is like digging through the earth until one gets to where diamonds are, it is trying to get deep spiritual things. We learn the deep things of God through meditation. 1 Corinthians 2:10 "But God hath revealed them unto us by his spirit: for the spirit searcheth all things, yea, the deep things of God."

Meaning of Meditation from a dictionary: "Penetrating or entering deeply into subjects of thought or thinking, having deep insight or understanding, penetrating to the depths of one's being." Reading the word only without meditation gives you information. Meditation changes the information that you have to become part of you, it then becomes life to you. During meditation the Holy Spirit transfers the information of the word of God to your spiritual mind from your natural mind. When the word from your mind meet in your spirit life is conceived. When the word gets into your spirit it affects your whole being spiritually and physically – it shifts your thinking system. Romans 12:2 "And be not conformed to this world: but be ye transformed by the renewing of your mind, that ye may prove what is that good, and acceptable, and perfect, will of God." Proverbs 4:20-22 "My son, attend to my words; incline thine ear unto my says. Let them not depart from thine eyes;

keep them in the midst of thine heart. For they are life unto those that find them, and health to all their flesh." When the word of God gets into your spirit through meditation it starts to affect you both spiritually, physically changing your life.

Whatever you meditate on takes total control of your life – this is what demons do when they build strongholds in one's life, they cause the person to think deeply on things that are contrary to the word of God. This is then transferred by demons into one's spirit and the person becomes what he has been meditating on. Proverbs 23:7 "For as he thinketh in his heart, so is he: Eat and drink, saith he to thee; but his heart is not with thee." This is why God says we should not be angry until the sun goes down because if we spend time meditating on our anger the devil will transfer the anger into your spirit and you will have a bitter life. Bitterness is harder to deal with than anger because it is a stronghold. Ephesians 4:26 "Be ye angry, and sin not: let not the sun go down upon your wrath." If one meditates on murder he will become a murderer.

Reading the word of God without meditation and you start to declare it, it does not work, that word has no power. Power comes when you are declaring it from your spirit through the power of the Holy Spirit, then there will be manifestations. All changes for children of God start from the spirit. When the word of God gets into your spirit you start to see things spiritually. What you see is so real as if you have the thing materially. It becomes so real and all doubt is driven out of you and you start to confess what you are seeing in your spirit as if it has already happened, and you have got no shadow of doubt in you. Hebrews 11:1 "Now faith is the substance of things hoped for, the evidence of things not seen." Things that are not seen in the physical are already seen in the spiritual and they are so real as though they were.

For the word of God to be effective in your life, it should not be kept in the mind. The mind is an enemy of the word of God. Romans 8:6-8 "For to be carnally minded is death; but to be spiritually minded is life and peace. Because the carnal mind is enmity against God: for it is not subject to the law of God, neither indeed can be. So, then they that are in the flesh cannot please God." The mind always wants to reason the word of God.

The mind stands for old wine skins, and the spirit stands for the new wine skins. Matthew 9:16-17 "No man putteth a piece of new cloth unto an old garment, for that which is put in to fill it up taketh from the garment, and the rent is made worse. Neither do men put new wine into old bottles: else the bottles break, and the wine runneth out, and the bottles perish: but they put new wine into new bottles, and both are preserved." The wine stands for the word of God. Your mind cannot contain the new wine because it is full of the doctrine of man. Matthew 15:9 "But in vain they do worship me, teaching for doctrines the commandments of men." Your spirit is the new wine skin which is able to contain the fermentation of the wine, the word of God. John 6:63 "It is The spirit that quickeneth; the flesh profiteth nothing: the words that I speak unto you, they are spirit, and they are life."

Immediately after hearing the word of God demons quickly come to take away the word of God before it is transferred into one's spirit. Matthew 13:4 "And when he sowed, some seeds fell by the way side, and the fowls came and devoured them up." The word of God is seed, and your spirit is the good ground. Your mind represents all the other types of bad soil. Matthew 13:3-8 "And he spake many things unto them in parables, saying, Behold, a sower went forth to sow; And when he sowed, some seeds fell by the way side, and the fowls came and devoured them up: Some fell upon stony places, where they had not much earth: and forthwith they sprang up, because they had no deepness of earth: and when the sun was up, they were scorched; and because they had no root, they withered away. And some fell among thorns; and the thorns sprung up, and chocked them: But other fell into good ground, and brought forth fruit, some an hundredfold, some sixtyfold, some thirtyfold." The mind is not the good ground for the word. When it gets into your mind, quickly transfer it through meditation into the good ground into your spirit. The word in your mind does not help you destroy strongholds.

Your spirit is not against the word of God because the word is also spirit. The moment the word gets into your spirit faith is born. When faith is born you are unstoppable, and no stronghold can stop you – all that seemed impossible becomes possible. Many children of God try to keep the word of God in their minds, but just knowing scriptures by heart does not help you. This is why people continue to be financially poor, yet they know scriptures that talk about financial prosperity, and people continue to be sick, yet they know scriptures about healing.

The more we study the word of God, the more we have the nature of Jesus Christ activated in us and strongholds cannot work when you have the new nature. They have their effectiveness in the old nature. Jacob wanted the blessing of God, yet he did not have the nature of God. God had to change him first, gave him his nature before blessing him. The name Jacob represented his old nature and Israel his new nature. Genesis 32:24-28 "And Jacob was left alone; and there wrestled a man with him until the breaking of the day. And when he saw that he prevailed not against him. He touched the hollow of his thigh, and the hollow of Jacob's thigh was out of joint, as he wrestled with him. And he said, let me go, for the day breaketh. And he said, I will not let thee go, except thou bless me. And he said unto him, what is thy name? And he said, Jacob. And he said, Thy name shall be called no more Jacob, but Israel: for as a prince hast thou power with God and with man, and hast prevailed."

Once we have the nature of God, strongholds are destroyed. As we continue in the word of God and developing the new nature the following starts happening in our lives. We start to see the world with the eyes of God. We understand who we are from God's point of view, that with God we can do all things. As this settles in our minds and our spirits well, strongholds are destroyed. The nature of God is supernatural it supersedes the power of strongholds and Knowing scriptures spiritually gives us the nature of God. Many Christians only know scriptures by their minds, that is why they are still under the control of strongholds. Yes, one could be born again but still being controlled by strongholds. To be born again is one thing but dealing with strongholds is another thing. When you get born again it's your spirit that gets born again and it's God who does that job. But after the birth it is your duty to deal with strongholds for you to be free indeed. John 8:31-32 "Then said Jesus to those Jews which believed on him, If ye continue in my word, then are ye my disciples indeed; And ye shall know the truth, and the truth shall make you free." Therefore, being born again is one thing but being free is another thing. I used to think that once born again all is done. Philippians 2:12 "Wherefore, my beloved, as ye have always obeyed, not as in my presence only, but now much more in my absence, work out your own salvation with fear and trembling." We must deal with the strongholds that are holding us from reaching to where God wants us to get to. The word of God is like fire and like a hammer, it burns down and breaks down every stronghold. Jeremiah 23:29 "Is not my word like as a fire? Saith the Lord; and like a hammer that breaketh the rock in pieces?"

How are Strongholds Destroyed?

The word of God adds value to your life – when you understand the word of God you understand your value and only God knows how valuable you are. All other people do not know your value, they are always devaluing you. Even yourself without the word of God, you do not know your value, and when you do not know your worth that is a big stronghold. If you meditate on teachings that are contrary to the word of God, you are feeding the strongholds and they become stronger. When you meditate on the truth of the word of God you weaken them and as a result they crumble, and they are destroyed.

Before destroying strongholds, you must first of all be delivered from all demons that are residing in you. Stop watching things on the television or internet that are of demonic origins – for example, pornography – and do not read materials that are satanic in nature. Continue to feed your mind with the truth of the word of God. Strongholds are not built in one day, they are built over a long period of time from the day that you are born. As a result, they are not weak structures they are very strong, stronger than the demons that build them. It is very easy to cast out a demon, but it is another thing to destroy a stronghold. It takes some minutes or hours to cast out a demon, but it takes weeks months and years to deal with strongholds. Many people think that once a demon is cast out, they are free. That is not true, that is only the beginning of getting free. This is why you find that some people when they get prayed for in church, they get healed but as soon as they go back home, they are sick again. The reason is that the demon of sickness was cast out at church, but the stronghold of sickness has not been destroyed.

As I said earlier on in the book, strongholds are not demons, but they are built by demons and demons use them to get in and out of the person. To cast out demons you just need the power of the Holy Spirit. To destroy strongholds, you need the power of the Holy Spirit and the word of God. Strongholds are built by the lies of the devil – they can only be destroyed by the renewal of the mind by the word of God. The renewal of the mind does not take one day – it is a journey, it is a long walk. When strongholds were being built it was also done stage by stage step by step. As you feed your spirit with the truth of the word of God believe it and start to act upon it, the way you used to act upon the lies of the devil. You will not get the results in one day or a few days, it takes time, but continue to feed your spiritual mind and doing what the word of God says. Step by step, strongholds are destroyed.

The devil still comes to you through your mind giving you doubt about the power that is in the word of God, and he tells you that it does not work. He distracts you from having quality time studying the word of God. You need the grace of God and commitment for you to be able to do the job otherwise you will leave it. Do not give up. The renewing of the mind is not done by God it is done by you and me. If we do not do it no one can do it for you, even your Pastor cannot do it for you. It is like breathing, no one can breathe for you, if you do not do it, you die.

Always think the word of God, speak the word of God and live the word of God, if you want strongholds to be destroyed. For example, the word of God says I am not a borrower but a lender. Deuteronomy 28:12 "The Lord shall open unto thee his good treasure, the heaven to give the rain unto thy land in his season, and to bless all the work of thine hand: and thou shalt lend unto many nations, and thou shalt be above only, and thou shalt not be beneath; If that thou hearken unto the commandments of the Lord thy God, which I command thee this day, to observe and to do them." Isaiah 54:5-7 "No weapon that is formed against thee shall prosper; and every tongue that shall rise against thee in judgement thou shalt condemn. This is the heritage of the servants of the lord, and their righteousness is me, saith the Lord." Matthew 17:20 "And Jesus said unto them, because of your unbelief: for verily I say unto you, If ye have faith as a grain of mustard seed, ye shall say unto this mountain, Remove hence to yonder place; and it shall remove; and nothing shall be impossible unto you." Isaiah 53:5 "But he was wounded for our transgressions, he was bruised for our iniquities: the chastisement of our peace was upon him; and with his stripes we are healed." We are called to live a life of abundance John 10:10 "The thief cometh not, but for to steal, and to kill, and to destroy; I am come that they might have life, and that they might have it more abundantly." The word of God is a powerful weapon to destroy strongholds.

Strongholds are so numerous, but in this book, I have only dealt with a few of them. Your destiny is in how you are going to deal with strongholds. They are the ones holding you back from your destiny. I think you can see why many children of God are struggling in life, yet they have the word of God full of promises. They are not dealing with strongholds – just going to church and doing all other church activities cannot transform them unless they deliver themselves. The bible says if a man is in Christ, he is a new creature, but if you do not deal with strongholds you will not see the newness in your life. 2 Corinthians 5:17 "Therefore if any man be in Christ, he is a new creature: old things are passed away; behold, all things are become new."

To destroy strongholds, change the way you think, change your mindset by the word of God. Change how you talk, talk like Jesus, Jesus spoke the word of God and have the character of Christ. Put off the old man and his ways. Your thoughts can change everything about your life. You are a product of how you think in your heart. When you want to live a victorious life, you have to live in the atmosphere of victory in your mind first. You cannot have thoughts of failure and live a successful life. When you speak the word of God coming out of your spirit filled with the power of the Holy Spirit what you say will come to pass. Stop believing teachings and beliefs that are contrary to the word of God.

You are what you are today because you believed what people told you, and you are what you are because of what you told yourself that you were. You are not what you think you are or what people say that you are but you are what God says that you are through his word. The devil knows the power that your mind has over your life, that is why he is busy corrupting it every day so that you may have corrupt results. He is not ill informed about you, he knows you pretty well in and out, but unfortunately you do not know anything about your life, who you are, where you are coming from and where you are going, your purpose, why God send you on earth. If the devil did not corrupt our minds, we should be doing exploits on earth. Just see how much strides man is still making with his corrupt mind, all the wonderful inventions that he has done and is still doing. It proves beyond doubt that he was created in the image of God.

Faith
Faith is paramount in the work of destroying strongholds. Faith is simply believing in God and acting upon every word that God says to us and obeying every instruction from Him. Our victories are a result of our obedience to the word of God. Abraham came out of the strongholds of his country and of his father's house through faith. Genesis 12:1-4 "Now the Lord said unto Abraham get thee out of thy country, and from thy kindred, and from thy father's house, unto a land that I will shew thee: And I make of thee a great nation, and I will bless thee, and make thy

name great; and thou shalt be a blessing: and I will bless them that bless thee, and curse him that curseth thee: and in thee shall all families of the earth be blessed. So Abram departed, as the Lord had spoken unto him; and Lot went with him and Abram was seventy five years old when he departed out of Haran." Without faith no stronghold can be broken.

As children of God, we have our victories through faith and we overcome strongholds by faith. 1 John 5:4 "For whatsoever is born of God overcometh the world: and this is the victory that overcometh the world, even our faith." The world that is in us through strongholds we overcome it by faith, faith is a walk, not a jump. It is life that must be lived every day not sometimes or on occasion. 2 Corinthians 5:7 "For we walk by faith, not by sight." Hebrews 10:38 "Now the just shall live by faith: but if any man draw back, my soul shall have no pleasure in him." Faith makes all things possible even pulling down of every stronghold in my life. Mark 9:23 "Jesus said unto him, If thou canst believe, all things are possible to him that believeth." Faith is imparted in a man by the word of God, therefore we must understand the word of God spiritually in order for us to have faith. Romans 10:17 "So then faith cometh by hearing and hearing by the word of God."

Many children of God are faithful but do not have faith. What do I mean? Many Christians are faithful to their church and church programs but they do not have faith from the word of God. They are considered faithful by other men, but they are not faithful to God. It's good to be faithful but strongholds cannot be destroyed by being faithful only, we need faith in God. This is why many of us complain to God many times and say, God see how I have been faithful towards you. Hebrews 11:6 "But without faith it is impossible to please him: for he that cometh to God must believe that he is, and that he is a rewarder of them that diligently seek him." You may be faithful to your church and yet continue to live bound by strongholds, and this is the state of many Christians today. Every Sunday they are at church, but they do not take the word of God seriously, they do not live the word. They are considered very faithful by their Pastor because every day when they are wanted at church, they are there. This is good, but without faith in God, it is a snare of the devil. God does not want us to put all things into his hands – there are things he has put into our hands. It is our work to deal with strongholds. 2 Timothy 4:7-8 "I have fought a good fight, I have finished my course, I have kept the faith." What transforms your life is faith, you have to fight by faith.

People without faith are full of fear and the absence of faith brings fear into action. We have seen that fear is a stronghold and there is no way one can destroy the stronghold of fear without faith. Faith is not afraid of anything and faith knows no failure. Hebrews 11:27-35 "By faith he forsook Egypt, not fearing the wrath of the king: for he endured, as seeing him who is invisible. Through faith he kept the Passover, and the sprinkling of blood, lest he that destroyed the firstborn should touch them. By faith they passed through the Red sea as by dry land: which the Egyptians assaying to do were drowned. By faith the walls of Jericho fell down, after they were compassed about seven days. By faith the harlot Rahab perished not with the spies with peace. And what shall I more say? For the time would fail me to tell of Gedeon, and Barak, and Samson, and Jephthae; and David also, and Samuel, and of the prophets: Who through faith subdued kingdoms, wrought righteousness, obtained promises, stopped the mouths of lions, quenched the violence of fire, escaped the edge of the sword, out of weakness were made strong, waxed valiant in fight, turned to fight the armies of the aliens: Women received their dead raised to life again: and others were tortured, not accepting deliverance; that they might obtain a better resurrection."

We need faith to be able to enter into the spiritual realm. Strongholds are spiritual – we need spiritual weapons to destroy them. 2 Corinthians 10:3-4 "For though we walk in the flesh, we do not war after the flesh: For the weapons of our warfare are not canal, but mighty through God to the pulling down of strongholds." Faith ushers us into the supernatural life of God, and it gives us ability to live above the systems of this world, the strongholds, demons, the devil and all that is controlling the world and its people. Faith gives us sight to see beyond the visible. People without faith cannot see the strongholds that are holding them back in their lives, to them all is well. They do not have spiritual eyes to see spiritual things. Strongholds are destroyed by people who have a very close relationship with God and without faith one cannot have a close relationship with God.

Strongholds can only be dealt with by people who have got faith in God – people who are not afraid of what they see. Faith does not hide from facts and facts cannot stop faith. Faith goes beyond facts and overrides facts, faith is not afraid of strongholds. 1 Samuel 17:4-8 "And there went out a champion out of the camp of the Philistines, named Goliath, of Gath, whose height was six cubits and a span. And he had an helmet of brass upon his head, and he was armed with a coat of mail; and the weight of the coat was five thousand shekels of brass. And he had greaves of brass upon his legs, and a target of brass between his shoulders. And the staff of his spear was like a weaver's bcam; and his spear's head weighed six hundred shekels of iron: and one bearing a shield went before him. And he stood and cried unto the armies of Israel, and said unto them, why are ye come out to set your battle in array? Am not I a Philistines, and ye servants to Saul? Choose you a man for you and let him come down to me." David was faced with facts, but those facts did not stop him.

Faith gives us one-hundred-percent belief, confidence, and trust in God. Strongholds cannot be broken unless we have belief, confidence, and trust in God. The presence of faith is the presence of the power of God that is needed to destroy strongholds. 1 Corinthians 4:20 "For the kingdom of God is not in word but in power." Faith ushers us into the glory realm, the realm of God, where all things are possible. When we operate in that realm every stronghold cannot stand but they will fall. Mark 10:27 "And Jesus looking upon them saith, with men it is impossible, but not with God all things are possible."

God is the glory, and the glory of God is God himself and the glory is His fullness, it is His manifest presence. His presence is glorious and nothing that is of satanic origin can stand in His glory. His glory is his presence, His character, His nature, and His ability, His provision and weight and splendour of His majesty. The glory is the essence of His beauty, He wants us to know Him in his totality and if we know Him thus no stronghold can remain standing in our lives. Psalm 138:5 "Yea they shall sing in the ways of the Lord: for great is the glory of the Lord." Acts 7:2 "And he said, men, brethren, and fathers, hearken; The God of glory appeared unto our father Abraham, when he was in Mesopotamia, before he dwelt in Charran."

Faith takes you to the blessings of Abraham thus destroying the stronghold of poverty. Galatians 3:9 "So then they which be of faith are blessed with faithful Abraham." Faith makes me whole, connects me to power, wealth, health, all the prosperity that God has promised us through His word, thus destroying every stronghold in my life. Luke 17:19 "And he said unto him, arise, go thy way: thy faith hath made thee whole." Faith restores what the devil has stolen from us through strongholds. Joel 2:25 "And I will restore to you the years that the locust hath eaten, the cankerworm, and the caterpillar, and the palmerworm, my great army which I sent among you." John 10:10 "The thief cometh but for to steal, and to kill and to destroy: I am come that they might have life, and that they might have it more abundantly."

In order to be able to destroy strongholds accept the promises of God by faith. Hebrews 11:13-14 "These all died in faith, not having received the promises, but having seen them afar off, and were persuaded of them, and embraced them, and confessed that they were strangers and pilgrims on the earth. For they that say such things declare plainly that they seek a country." Renounce all confidence in human resources and have confidence in God. Romans 4:18-21 "Who against hope believed in hope, that he might become the father of many nations; according to that which was spoken, so shall thy seed be. And being not weak in faith, he considered not his own body now dead, when he was about hundred years old, neither yet the deadness of Sara's womb: He staggered not at the promise of God through unbelief; but was strong in faith, giving glory to God; And being fully persuaded that, what he had promised, he was able to also to perform." We must focus on God and his promises by faith then all strongholds will be destroyed.

Rest on God's faithfulness. Do not look at your weaknesses as you are destroying the strongholds, it is not about your ability but the ability of God. Your biggest job is to have faith in God, and he will do the rest. It was not the promises of Abraham that mattered but God. Abraham thanked God before the child was born. Faith and praise are inseparable, praising God in faith has power to destroy strongholds. Joshua 6:20 "So the people shouted when the priests blew with the trumpets: and it came to pass, when the people heard the sound of the trumpet, and the people shouted with a great shout, that the wall fell down flat, so that the people went up into the city, every man straight before him, and they took the city." Praise is the highest expression to God, when we praise God the presence and the glory of God comes down. When the glory comes down every stronghold in your life will be broken and destroyed. John 8:36 "If the Son therefore shall make you free, ye shall be free indeed."

The Blood of Jesus Christ
The blood of JESUS remits sin and washes our sins away. Matthew 26:28 "For this is my blood of the new testament, which is shed for many for the remission of sins." A man in his sins, not born again does not have the capacity to destroy strongholds, he needs power to do that. John 1:12 "But as many as received him, to them gave he power to become the sons of God, even to them that believe on his name." The blood of Jesus Christ liberates man from the power of sin, the devil and his demons. Revelation 12:10 "And they overcame him by the blood of the lamb, and the word of their testimony; and they loved not their lives unto death."

I am made one with Christ and dwell in him through the Blood of Jesus Christ. John 6:56 "He that eateth my flesh, and drinketh my blood, dwelleth in me, and I in him." If I am not in Christ, there is no way that I may be able to destroy strongholds. Through the blood of Jesus Christ, I am justified and saved from the wrath of God. Romans 5:9 "Much more then, being justified by his blood, we shall be saved from the wrath of him." There is no way I can destroy strongholds if I am under the wrath of God. Without the blood of Jesus Christ, I am an alien and a foreigner from the commonwealth of Israel even to the things of God. The blood of Jesus Christ has brought me near to God and made me a member of the household of God. Ephesians 2:11-13 "Wherefore remember, that ye being in the time past Gentiles in the flesh, who are called Uncircumcision by that which is called the Circumcision in the flesh made by hands; That at that time ye were without Christ, being aliens from the commonwealth of Israel and strangers from the covenants of promise, having no hope, and without God in the world: But now in Christ Jesus ye who sometimes were far off are made nigh by the blood of Christ." Only those in the household of God have the capacity and ability to destroy strongholds.

The blood of Jesus Christ cleanses us from dead works to serve the living God. Hebrews 9:14 "How much more shall the blood of Christ, who through the eternal Spirit offered himself without spot to God, purge your conscience from dead works to serve the living God." Sin empowers strongholds, therefore if you are not cleansed and you are still in your sins you cannot destroy strongholds. You can enter into the holy of holies with boldness through and only through the blood of Christ. Hebrews 10:19 "Having therefore, brethren, boldness to enter into the holiest by the blood of Jesus." It is when we are in the holy of holies that we are in the presence of God and no stronghold can stand the glory of God. In the holy of holies every stronghold is rendered useless. When in the presence of God all that is not of God is destroyed and is replaced by the life of God and the plan of God. Every plan of the devil is destroyed in the presence of God and the blood of Jesus grants us forgiveness. Colossians 1:14 "In whom we have redemption through his blood, even the forgiveness of sins." Without the forgiveness of sins, it is impossible to destroy strongholds. Strongholds are built upon sin and lies of the devil. Unforgiveness empowers strongholds that are in my life. When God forgives me of my sins, I am empowered to destroy strongholds.

Prayer and Fasting
Prayer and fasting gives us victories and there are some situations that need prayer and fasting for them to change. Strongholds need prayer and fasting for their destructions. Matthew 17:15-21 "Lord, have mercy on my son: for he is lunatic, and sore vexed: for oftentimes he falleth into the fire, and into the water. And I brought him to thy disciples, and they could not cure him. Then Jesus answered and said, O faithless and perverse generation, how long shall I be with you? how long shall I suffer you? Bring him thither to me. And Jesus rebuked the devil; and he departed out of him: and the child was cured from that very hour. Then came the disciples to Jesus apart, and said, why could not we cast him out? And Jesus said unto them, Because of your unbelief: verily I say unto you, If you have faith as a grain of a mustard seed, ye shall say unto this mountain, Remove hence to yonder place; and it shall remove; and nothing shall be impossible unto you. Howbeit this kind goeth not out but by prayer and fasting."

Yokes of strongholds are broken by prayer and fasting. Isaiah 10:27 "And it shall come to pass in that day, that his burden shall be taken away from off thy shoulder, and his yoke from off thy neck, and the yoke shall be destroyed because of the anointing." Every bondage is a yoke and every stronghold is a yoke which must be broken. A stronghold does not allow you to progress in life, It keeps you tied at one spot. Luke 19:30-31 "Saying, go ye into the village over against you; in the which at your entry ye shall find a colt tied, whereon yet never man sat: loose him, and bring him hither. And if any man asks you, Why do ye loose him? Thus shall ye say unto him, because the Lord hath need of Him." You have to loose yourself from strongholds through prayer and fasting.

The time we are in the presence of God in prayer there is

impartation taking place which destroys strongholds. Prayer and fasting brings us into the shekinah glory of God. Exodus 34:29 "And it came to pass, when Moses came down from mount Sinai with the two tables of testimony in Moses' hand, when he came down from the mount, that Moses wist not that the skin of his face shone while he talked with him. And when Aaron and all the children of Israel saw Moses, behold, the skin of his face shone; and they were afraid to come nigh him."

Prayer and fasting subdues the flesh, if you follow your flesh you miss many things pertaining to the kingdom of God which is a spiritual kingdom. Strongholds are built by demons through the flesh and the strongholds are destroyed by the spirit of God. Romans 8:13 "For if ye live after the flesh, ye shall die: but if ye through the spirit do mortify the deeds of the body, ye shall live. We get the things of God which are spiritual not through flesh and blood but through the spirit." 1 Corinthians 15:45-50 "And so it is written, The first man Adam was made a living soul; the last Adam was made a quickening spirit. Howbeit that was not first which is spiritual, but that which is natural; and afterward that which is spiritual. The first man is of the earth, earthly: the second man is the Lord from heaven. As is the earthly, such are they also that are earthly: and as is the heavenly, such are they also that are heavenly. And as we have borne the image of the earthly, we shall also bear the image of the heavenly. Now this I say, brethren, that flesh and blood cannot inherit the kingdom of God; neither doth corruption inherit incorruption." People who do not know what is happening in their lives usually do not see any reason why they should fast and pray. They are blind and they are comfortable with the status core. People who are not aware that they have strongholds in their lives do not see any need to fast and pray. People who are spiritually blind cannot pray. When one is dead spiritually, he thinks all is well with him, yet everything is wrong. 2 Kings 6:17 "And Elisha prayed, and said, Lord I pray thee, open his eyes, that he may see. And the Lord opened the eyes of the young man; and he saw: and, behold, the mountain was full of horses and chariots of fire round about Elisha."

People who have discovered strongholds in their lives are desperate for change and they go to God in desperation through prayer and fasting. They know that it is only God who can save them, and they go to him. Esther 4:16 "Go gather together all the Jews that are present in Shushan, and fast ye for me, and neither eat nor drink three days, night or day: I also and my maidens will fast likewise; and so will go in unto the king, which is not according to the law: and if I perish, I perish." This is the attitude of a person who is dealing with strongholds.

If you understand that strongholds can only be destroyed by the power of God, you will engage in serious prayer and fasting. David understood that his victories were only with the Lord that is why he prayed to God. Nothing can set us free from the power of strongholds except God. Samuel 30:1-6 "And it came to pass, David and his men were come to Ziglag on the third day, and smitten had invaded the south, and Ziklag, and smitten Ziklag, and burned it with fire; And had taken the women captives, that were therein: they slew not any, either great or small, but carried them away, and went on their way. So, David and his men came to the city, and, behold, it was burned with fire and their wives, and their sons, and their daughters, were taken captives. Then David and the people that were with him lifted up their voice and wept, until they had no power to weep. And David's two wives were taken captives Ahinoam the Jezraelitess, and Abigail the wife of Nabal the Carmelite. And David was greatly distressed; for the people spake of stoning him, because the soul of all the people was grieved, every man for his sons and for his daughters: but David encouraged himself in the Lord his God."

There is power in prayer and fasting to destroy strongholds. James 5:15-16 "And the prayer of faith shall save the sick, and the Lord shall raise him up; and if he has committed sins, they shall be forgiven him. Confess your faults one to another, and pray one for another, that ye may be healed. The effectual fervent prayer of a righteous man availeth much." With prayer and fasting situations are changed and mountains are moved. Elijah prayed and for three years it did not rain. James 5:17 "Elias was a man subject to like passions as we are, and he prayed earnestly that it might rain: and it rained not on the earth by space of three years and six months." The children of Israel at one time were supposed to be killed, all of them, but through prayer and fasting the opposite happened. Esther 9:1-2,5 "Now in the twelfth month, that is the moth Adar, on the thirteenth day of the same, when the king's commandment and his decree drew near to be put in execution, in the day that the enemies of the Jews hoped to have power over them, (though it was turned to the contrary, that the Jews had rule over them that hated them;) Thus the Jews smote all their enemies with the stroke of the sword, and slaughter, and destruction, and did what they would unto those that hated them."

Without intensive prayer strongholds continue to hold you back and haunt your life. This is why the devil distracts people from praying. Prayer and fasting have incredible power to arrest, stop and nullify the purposes of the devil. Prayer must be part of your life and live in the attitude of prayer. To pray effectively you must always live in an attitude of prayer. When you pray in the spirit and speak the word of God you will be tearing down strongholds in your life and the deeper things of God are learnt during prayer. As you are learning those deeper things the Holy

Spirit will be working through the word of God to tear down every imagination that exalts itself above the truth of the word of God in your mind.

There is no substitute for prayer in the pulling down of strongholds. Prayer is a great spiritual force in the pulling down of strongholds. "I believe the power of fasting as it relates to prayer is the spiritual atomic bomb that our Lord has given us to destroy the strongholds of evil and usher in a great revival and spiritual harvest around the world." Bill Bright, *7 Steps to Successful Fasting and Prayer*, www.cru.org/train-ing-and growth/devotional-life/7-steps-to-fasting/index.htm. Prayer, fasting and holy life are very important, they act and react mutually to the pulling down of strongholds. As I continue fellowshipping with the heavenly Father in the spirit, strongholds are weakened and as I continue the fellowship on daily basis, it becomes part of my life, strongholds are continuously weakened until they are destroyed.

The Name of Jesus Christ

Every demon, every devil, anything that has a name in heaven or on earth cannot stand against the name of Jesus Christ. When the name of Jesus Christ is spoken by faith no stronghold can stand. Continue to speak the name of Jesus Christ to those strongholds by faith and they will fall. "You are to destroy strongholds in the name of Jesus Christ. At the name of Jesus, satan will flee and spiritual strongholds will be obliterated, regardless of their apparent strength. Activate the power of God by using the weapon of the name of Jesus." Ronnie Floyd, *How to Pray*, Thomas Nelson Inc, 18/06/1999, page 141.

There is power in the name of Jesus in the tearing down of strongholds. However, the name of Jesus Christ does not work if you do not live a holy life. When the name of Jesus Christ is called upon by a holy man it has incredible power, it can heal the sick, raise the dead and change every situation. There is nothing that has got power to resist the name of Jesus Christ even strongholds. Strongholds and the strongman crumble when they hear the name that is above every name, the name of Jesus Christ. Continue to speak the name of Jesus Christ and the stronghold will be destroyed. "Every stronghold of confusion erected against me, I pull you down today, be destroyed by the fire of God." Timothy Atunnise, *Earth-Moving Prayers: Pray Until Miracle Happens*, Booktango, 02/07/2013, page 42. The devil knows fully well that he was defeated at Calvary by Jesus Christ, he was rendered powerless and was disarmed forever. He only uses the ignorance of people that is why he appears as if he has power. Colossians 2:15 "And having spoiled principalities and power, he made a shew of them openly, triumphing over them in it."

The name of Jesus Christ carries power, victory and authority above all powers that are in heaven and on earth. Unless one is a born-again, child of God, the name of Jesus does not work. Only children of God can use the name of Jesus Christ and get results. Acts 16:18 "And this did she many days. But Paul, being grieved, turned and said to the spirit, I command thee in the name of Jesus Christ to come out of her. And he came out the same hour." When you call upon the name of Jesus Christ strongholds are shaken and destroyed. However, the destruction does not happen in a single day. As I said earlier on in the book, destroying strongholds is progressive, it is not a one-day job, it is progressive.

Before you embark on destroying strongholds, identify the stronghold – you need to know them first otherwise you cannot fight with something that you do not know. The devil does not want you to know the strongholds that he has built in your life.

He wants you to think that whatever is happening in your life is just but normal, you need the help of the Holy Spirit to identify them.

The Holy Spirit
Without the Holy Spirit all other weapons are not effective – they are only effective through the power of the Holy Spirit. Prayer without the power of the Holy Spirit is useless. Romans 8:26 "Likewise the Spirit also helpeth our infirmities: for we know not what we should pray for as we ought: but the spirit itself maketh intercession for us with groanings which cannot be uttered. The blood of Jesus Christ that was shed two thousand years ago is effective through the power of the Holy Spirit. The word of God is ineffective without the power of the Holy Spirit. The fivefold ministry gifts cannot work without the Holy Spirit. Ephesians 4:11 And he gave some, apostles; and some, prophets; and some, evangelists; and some, pastors and teachers."

Everything about God and the kingdom of God is propelled and is moved by the power of the Holy Spirit. Therefore, it follows that for someone to be able to destroy strongholds that are in his life it is of paramount importance for him to be filled by the Holy Spirit, he must have the power and the fire of the Holy Spirit. Matthew 3:11 "I indeed baptize you with water unto repentance: but he that cometh after me is mightier than I, whose shoes I am not to bear: he shall baptize you with the Holy Ghost, and with fire." Without the Holy Spirit the task of destroying strongholds is impossible.

Strongholds are built in the minds of people because of the absence of the Holy Spirit in them. Man was not meant to live without the Holy Spirit in operation in his life, this is why there is so much suffering and turmoil in the world today. When God created man in the beginning, He never intended him to live without the Holy Spirit. The Holy Spirit is the operational power of God through whom he does all things. Without the power of the Holy Spirit no stronghold can be shaken, and nothing can shake it.

The Holy Spirit is indispensable in the pulling down of strongholds. Strongholds cannot be destroyed by just mere men, but only by men and women who are endued with power of the Holy Spirit. Acts 1:8 "But ye shall receive power, after that the Holy Ghost is come upon you: and ye shall be witnesses unto me both in Jerusalem, and in all Judea, and in Samaria, and unto the uttermost part of the earth." It demands supernatural power of the Holy Spirit to destroy strongholds. 1 Corinthians 4:20 "For the kingdom of God is not in word, but in power." There are so many people who are trying to change things happening in their lives but are failing because they do not have the Holy Spirit at work in their lives. Man needs the never-failing power of the Holy Spirit in his life. Man is made into a new creature by the power of the Holy Spirit at work in him. 2 Corinthians 5:17 "Therefore if any man be in Christ, he is a new creature: old things are passed away; behold, all things are become new." It is only the new man who can destroy strongholds. The Holy Spirit gives us access to God and without this access no man can deal with strongholds. Strongholds are dealt with when we are in the presence of God in the holy of holies having fellowship with our heavenly Father.

Faith is a necessity to destroy strongholds and if you do not have the Holy Spirit you cannot have faith. The Holy Spirit gives us the ability to walk in the spirit and to operate in the spirit. The work of destroying strongholds is spiritual because strongholds are spiritual. Strongholds are built in human mind by satanic spirits therefore it takes the Holy Spirit to destroy them.

The Fivefold Ministry

You need the help of the fivefold ministry to destroy strongholds in your mind. Ephesians 4:11-12 "And he gave some, apostles; and some, prophets; and some evangelists; and some pastors and teachers; For the perfecting of the saints, for the work of the ministry, for the edifying of the body of Christ." These people have been put into your life by God so that they may continue in the work of perfecting you. As you allow them to operate in your life you are allowing God to continue liberating you from the grip of the devil through strongholds. You need the foundation that is laid upon by Apostles and Prophets. Ephesians 2:19-20 "Now therefore ye are no more strangers and foreigners, but fellowcitizens with the saints, and of the household of God; and are built upon the foundation of the apostles and prophets, Jesus Christ being the chief corner stone..." Humble yourself under their leadership. The foundation that they lay in your life through the word of God has the power to destroy strongholds. You need an Evangelist to deliver you from demonic oppressions and possessions. "The ministry gift of exorcism is the supernaturally empowered ability which God gives to certain members of the body of Christ to use their gifts to destroy demonic strongholds in the lives of other believers" Mark Stewart, *Releasing the Power of Your Spiritual Gifts*, iUniverse, 2002, page 339.

The Pastor is a shepherd – his work is to nurture you and to help you grow in the knowledge of God, and as he nurtures you to maturity strongholds are destroyed. The ministry gift of a teacher grounds you in the true knowledge of the word of God. Strongholds are built through false teachings therefore, the teacher is very important he teaches you the truth of the word of God which in turn destroy the strongholds. You knock down strongholds by the word of God. John 8:32 "And ye shall know the truth, and the truth shall make you free." Receive every ministry gift into your life it has a godly purpose of setting you free. You cannot do it alone you need these men and women of God to help you.

CHAPTER 5

CONCLUSION

Going to heaven is not a problem, the biggest problem that children of God face is to manage and dominate the forces of darkness that are at work in this world and in their lives – we cannot function and manifest the kingdom of God if we do not change our mindset. We must utterly destroy the strongholds that are holding us captive. The devil is unleashing his attacks upon the children of God from their minds through the strongholds. People are born again but their minds are not born again – it is the spirit that is born again.

Christians can sing songs of victory at church but that is not what they live at home. Things are not changing in their lives because they have not yet changed their mindset. If your mind is under attack, there is no change that can take place. Christianity is more of a talk than a walk to many. Many are oppressed and suppressed by strongholds. Man was created in the image of God and in His likeness but because of sin everything has gone wrong with him. Jesus came to put man to his original position, but man has to understand how he can be restored. The restoration process involves God and man – for example, God does not destroy strongholds for you – you must do it yourself. Philippians 2:12 "Wherefore, my beloved, as ye have always obeyed, not as in my presence only, but now much more in my absence, work out your own salvation with fear and trembling." There is no way children of God can dominate the devil if their way of thinking is not different from his. The word of God gives us a new mindset.

To manifest the kingdom of God we must have a kingdom of God mindset, a new thinking system must be put in place and Children of God must have a Christ mindset. Many Christians are like the children of Israel – they were out of Egypt physically yet in their minds they were still in Egypt – they kept their old mentality and their way of doing things. Instead of getting a new mentality, the godly mentality and the new way of doing things they clang to their Egyptian mentality. Numbers 11:5-6 "We remember the fish, which we did eat in Egypt freely; the cucumbers, and the melons, and the leeks, and the onions, and the garlic: But now our soul is dried away: there is nothing at all beside this manna, before our eyes." They did not embrace the new life that God had given them, and all of them perished in the desert. It was only Caleb and Joshua who made it into the promised land because they thought differently and saw things differently. Only those who were born in the desert made it to the promised land, why because they were a new generation that knew nothing of Egypt. The new generation had no Egyptian strongholds – they only knew the God of miracles whom they saw in the desert, and they embraced Him fully.

Strongholds are holding people back from enjoying what God has prepared for us. The devil is not worried when people just go to church but without change. It does not matter how much we may talk about God if we are not pulling down strongholds the devil is still in charge and in control and that is his joy. After coming to the Lord and you continue to think, talk, live, and see the same way that you did before coming to Christ, then you are still under the oppression of the devil. Some are satisfied because they have stopped stealing and lying, they think all is well with them. You cannot live a victorious kind of life if you have strongholds.

Many times, before the devil uses someone in a certain way, he builds a stronghold in his mind. He will use that stronghold to enter into his life every time when he wants to use him or afflict him, and the mind is the door or the point of contact of the devil into your life. If there is no stronghold in your mind the devil has no power over, you.

What a person hears very often, see, read, talk about, the devil uses that to build strongholds. If what you see often is of satanic origins e.g. pornography, a stronghold of sexual immorality is built in your mind without you realising it. After some time, you will find out that you are hooked to sexual immorality. Your mind gets conditioned to it, you will always think of it. Images of pornography are always running up and down in your mind even if you do not want to think about it, you lose control of your mind to it, and it dominates your mind, it controls you. What you see often and think about that is what you become, you are what you see, hear, read. "We have polluted the minds of young with pornography, until crime and sexual assaults are now commonplace." Tim Lahaye and David Noebel, *Mind Siege*, page 48.

If your mind is dominated by pornography it means that is what you become. David slept with Uriah's wife because he saw what he was not supposed to see – as he was watching Uriah's wife washing her body, he was exposing himself to the devil. When he saw he was supposed to leave at once, but he did not leave he continued to have a good look at the nude woman. As he was taking that good look the devil built a stronghold in his mind, and when he went back into his house, he kept on thinking about the woman he saw, until he could not control himself, he had to send someone to bring her to him and he slept with her.

2 Samuel 11:2-4 "And it came to pass in an eveningtide, that David arose from off his bed, and walked upon the roof of the king's house: and from the roof he saw a woman washing herself; and the woman was very beautiful to look upon. And David sent and enquired after the woman. And one said, is not this Bathsheba, the daughter of Elaim, the wife of Uriah the Hittite? And David sent messengers and took her; and she came in unto him, and he lay with her; for she was purified from her uncleanness: and she returned unto her house."

Some people say that they can see anything, they say they can control themselves, but that is a lie of the devil. If you want to have the right feelings, you must watch and hear the right things so that you can generate the right thoughts. "Our youth seem obsessed with sex because depraved adults are providing them with the pornographic fuel with which they burn up their lives." Tim Lahaye and David Noebel, *Mind Siege*, page 50.

If you want to live a victorious life believe the word, not what people say. If you hear things that instils fear, doubt into your life do not continue to hear it. Faith comes by hearing and by hearing the word of God. Doubt, which is the enemy of faith, also comes by hearing and hearing the word of demons and people. Many people today are what they are because of what they heard people say about them – some have been told that they will never be successful in life because they are not educated, and they have accepted it and they have become exactly that.

There is power in every word that is spoken, negative words are empowered by the devil. When they are spoken the devil is behind those words to make sure they are fulfilled. The word of God is empowered by God. Jeremiah 1:12 "Then said the Lord unto me, Thou hast well seen: for I will hasten my word to perform it." Words spoken whether negative or positive in people's lives, they do not just disappear they become part of the person to whom they have been spoken to – they mould the destiny of that person. Words spoken are not forgotten especially the bad ones. The devil always uses those words to remind you when he wants to affect and control your life and that is a stronghold.

Words are very powerful, they have started wars, they have caused divorces, they have separated very close friends. The word of God has transferred people from hell to heaven, has transformed people from poverty to prosperity. The word of God has set free men who were once under the oppression of the devil, has opened the eyes of blind people, the crippled have walked. The word of God has brought back life to dry bones, the word of God is life. Ezekiel 37:3-10 "And he said unto me, Son of man, can these bones live? And I answered, O Lord God, thou knowest. Again, he said unto me, Prophesy upon these bones, and say unto them, O ye dry bones, hear the word of the Lord. Thus saith the Lord God unto these bones; Behold, I will cause breath to enter into you, and ye shall live: And I will lay sinews upon you, and will bring up flesh upon you, and cover you with skin, and put breath in you, and ye shall live; and ye shall know that I am the Lord. So, I prophesied as I was commanded: and as I prophesied, there was a noise, and behold a shaking, and the bones came together, bone to his bone. And when I beheld, lo, the sinews and the flesh came up upon them, and the skin covered them above: but there was no breath in them. Then said he unto me, Prophesy unto the wind, prophesy, son of man, and say to the wind, Thus saith the Lord God; Come from the four winds, Obreath, and breath upon these slain, that they may live. So, I prophesied as he commanded me, and the breath came into them, and they lived, and stood up upon their feet, an exceeding great army."

The words of the devil bring death, do not listen to the voice of the devil, when he speaks to you, speak back to him the true word of God. When he speaks do not remain quiet, speak back the word of God. Matthew 4:3-4 "And when the tempter came to him, he said, If thou be the son of God, command that these stones be made bread. But he answered and said, It is written, man shall not live by bread alone, but by every word that proceedeth out of the mouth of God." When the devil speaks to you and you do not answer him it means you are agreeing with what he is saying. When Goliath spoke to David, David did not remain quiet he spoke back to the enemy. 1 Samuel 17:42-47 "And when the Philistine looked about, and saw David, he disdained him: for he was but a youth, and ruddy, and of a fair countenance. And the Philistine said unto David, Am I a dog, that thou comest to me with staves? And the Philistine cursed David by his Gods. And the Philistine said to David, Come to me, and I will give thy flesh unto the fowls of the air, and to the beasts of the field. Then said David to the Philistine, Thou comest to me with a sword, and with a spear, and with a shield: but I come to thee in the name of the Lord of hosts, the God of the armies of Israel, whom thou hast defied. This day will the Lord deliver thee into mine hand; and I will smite thee, and take thine head from thee; and I will give the carcases of the host of the Philistines this day unto the fowls of the air, and to the wild beasts of the earth; that all the earth may know that there is a God in Israel. And all this assembly shall know that the Lord saveth not with sword and spear: for the battle is the Lord's, and he will give you into our hands."

Strongholds are built through false and humanistic teachings, through literature and books etc. Every material that is written, has a spirit behind it. The writer may not know it, but the spirit that pushed the person to write knows exactly what it wants to achieve with the writing. The lies of the devil are spread very fast through literature. When people see a book, they cannot see the devil who is behind that book. Many books that are written by people who do not know God has the influence of the devil in them. There are some lies that are being transmitted through that book, for example, in some medical books there are some diseases that are grouped as terminal. This is a lie because according to the word of God there is no disease that cannot be cured. Psalm 103:3 "Who forgiveth all thine iniquities: who heals all thy diseases. The world has been made to believe that there are terminal diseases and people have accepted it."

There are many things that people can do but through certain books have been taught that those things are impossible to do. But the true word of God says that we can do all things through Christ who strengthens us. Philippians 4:13 "I can do all things through Christ which strengtheneth me." Many satanic lies and humanistic teachings are spread through books.

How a person speaks is a result of what is full in his heart. If the mind is full of negative thoughts of demons, the mouth will say just that and nothing more. Luke 6:45 "A good man out of the good treasure of his heart bringeth forth that which is good; and an evil man out of the evil treasure of his heart bringeth forth that which is evil: for of the abundance of the heart his mouth speaketh."

Man is created in the image of God therefore when he speaks, what he speaks will come to pass. If you speak negative things upon your life, they will come to pass. Proverbs 6:2 "Thou art snared with the words of thy mouth, thou art taken with the words of thy mouth." The negative things that you have said to yourself and what other people have said about you have become strongholds in your life.

Strongholds can operate in a person even when demons are

not present. Demons are not omnipresent; they move with time and from place to place. Strongholds are stronger than demons – they torment people more than demons because they are always with you, but demons are not always with you. You suffer more from a wrong mindset than you suffer under demons. The devil is interested in your mind than everything else. He is a strategist, he does not attack anyhow; he knows very well how a man functions – he knows how important the mind is, that is why his attacks are all pointed to the mind. Once he gets the mind, he has you under his control.

Everything that happens in your life is processed in your mind – if you fail, what it means is you failed first in your mind – what we see on the ground it started to happen in the mind. What we see physically is the manifest of what has been happening in the mind. If you are poor it means you are poor in your mind, you cannot be rich in your mind and be poor physically. The devil attacks your thinking system from every angle, once that is done its game over.

The most basic thing that the devil does not want you to discover is who you are; where you came from and your purpose. Once you are ignorant of these things, he has got you. Many people are born, and they die without knowing who they are and why they were brought into the world. It is easy to oppress and suppress someone who does not know who he is and his purpose. If man would discover that he was created by God and in his own image and in his likeness, he would not want to live any life that is less than that. Genesis 1:26-27 "And God said, let us make man in our image, after our likeness: and let them have dominion over the fish of the sea, and over the fowl of the air, and over the cattle, and over the fowl of the air, and over the cattle, and over all the earth, and over every creeping thing that creepeth upon the earth." When you get saved by Jesus Christ, your mind is not saved, you have to get it saved by destroying the strongholds and renewing it by the word of God. God does not save your mind it is your duty to save your mind by destroying strongholds. Your mind must align with your spirit that has been saved. If your mind is not saved it means, there is always a fight within you. Your spirit is speaking the word of God, but your mind is against what the spirit is saying. Romans 7:21 "I find then a law, that, when I would do good, evil is present with me. For I delight in the law of God after the inward man: But I see another law in my members, warring against the law of my mind, and bringing me into captivity to the law of sin which is my members." When your spirit man speaks your mind must say yes and amen.

Many people think that they were created to work in the companies that they are working in. Satan tells them that this is all about life. They work all the days of their lives and after many years go on pension, live a few years after that and die. Is that what life is all about, I say no. Satan does not give man time enough to sit down and discover who he is, he keeps him very busy with the issues of life. He is made to go up and down doing things that he thinks are very important, yet it is all but vanity. Ecclesiastes 1:1-8 "The words of the preacher, the son of David, king in Jerusalem. Vanity of vanities, saith the Preacher, vanity of vanities; all is vanity. What profit hath a man of all his labour which he taketh under the sun? One generation passeth away, and another generation cometh: but the earth abideth for ever. The sun also ariseth, and the sun goeth down, and hasteth, and the sun goeth down, and hasteth to his place where he arose. The wind goeth toward the south, and turneth about unto the north; it whirleth about continually, and the wind returneth again according to his circuits. All the rivers run into the sea; yet the sea is not full; unto the place from whence the rivers come, thither they return again; All l things are full of labour; man cannot utter it: the eye is not satisfied with seeing, nor the ear filled with hearing."

Principles of the kingdom of the devil are embedded in the minds of all men and women through strongholds that the devil and his demons have been building from the day a child is born. If the kingdom of God is to manifest in the lives of the children of God, it must start in their minds. There must be a dramatic revolution of the minds – there is no way one can become a new creation, yet he still has his old mindset. Just going to church and singing some songs cannot deliver us from the grip of the devil. The mind must be renewed and made new by the word of God. Without the renewal of the mind there is no new life in Christ.

BIBLIOGRAPHY AND REFERENCES

Timothy Atunnise, *Earth-Moving Prayers: Pray Until Miracle Happens*, Booktango, 02/07/2013

Ronnie Floyd, *How to Pray*, Thomas Nelson Inc, 18/06/1999

Robert H. Givons, *Preparing from a Christian Perpective: Superb Handbook for Successful Living*, AuthorHouse

Miriam Grossman, *You are Teaching My Child What?*, Regnery Publishing, 04/08/2009

Lizzy Iweala, *How to Identify and Destroy Evil Patterns in Your Life: Spiritual Warfare*, AuthorHouse, 19/11/2008

Alan Marzilli, *Religion in Public Schools*, Infobase Publishing, 01/01/2009

James Padget, James E. Padgett (recorder), Lulu com, 21/07/2008

Vermon Sparks, *Child Age Education*, Digital inspiration, 1995

Dr Ray Stedman, *Spiritual Warefare Book 4: Winning the Daily Battle with Satan*.

Pulling Down of Strongholds

Mark Allan Stewart, *Releasing the Power of Your Spiritual Gifts*, iUniverse, 2002

Preston Tolliver, *What the Bible Says*, Trafford Publishing, 2009

Christine Van Horn, *God in Schools*, Xulon Press, 2010

Wangula E, *Traditional Leaders on the Frontline*, 2012, pdf retrieved from www4health.org/default/fies/SAFAIDS Addressing Harmful Cultural Practices.

Other References: Books written by more than one person

David Lahaye and David Noebel, *Mind Siege*, Colorado Springs Publishing, 2012

Jagdeep S Chhokar, Felix C Brodbeck, Robert J House, *Culture and Leadership Across the World: The GLOBE Book of In-Depth Studies*, Psychology Press, 12/02/2007

Lawrence Harrison, Samuel Huntington, *Culture Matters*, Basic Books, 2000

References from the Internet

www.Cru.org/training-and growth/devotional-life/7-steps-to-fasting/index.htm

Heuristic (2012) in Collins online dictionary retrieved from www.CollinsDictionary.com/dictionary/ English/stronghold

ABOUT THE AUTHOR

Dr Francis Madzivadondo is a seasoned Pastor, ordained in 1990, after three years of training in Biblical Studies and Christian Leadership at Africa Multination For Christ College (AMFCC) in Zimbabwe Africa, a bible college for Forward In Faith Ministries International Church.

He holds the following qualifications:

- Diploma in Biblical studies and Christian Leadership from (AMFCC)
- Diploma in Community Services – Australia
- Advanced Diploma Counselling and Psychology – International Careers Institute – Australia
- Bachelor's Degree in Christian Education
- Master's Degree in Christian Education
- Doctor of Philosophy in Christian Education – Newburgh Theological College USA

He is an international Gospel conference and television speaker, has Pastored in many places around Zimbabwe before being sent out to many other countries as a short term and long term missionary, Mozambique, South Africa, Democratic Republic of Congo (DRC), South Pacific Islands of Tonga, Australia, Canada, USA, Belize, United Kingdom.

Pulling Down of Strongholds

When the book was written, he was the National Administrator/ National Overseer of Forward In Faith Ministries International in New Zealand.

He is the author of Kingdom of God – Marriage Dynamics.

Before answering to the call of God to ministry Dr Francis was an Administrator Finance and Personnel in the government of Zimbabwe. He is married to Pastor Sandra and together they have five children.

www.ingramcontent.com/pod-product-compliance
Lightning Source LLC
Chambersburg PA
CBHW071407290426
44108CB00014B/1724